ESSAYS IN CRITICISM

SECOND SERIES

BY

MATTHEW ARNOLD

MACMILLAN AND CO., LIMITED
ST. MARTIN'S STREET, LONDON

1925

COPYRIGHT

First published 1888
First Pocket Edition 1925

PRINTED IN GREAT BRITAIN

PREFATORY NOTE

THE collection of Essays contained in this volume was made by Mr. Arnold himself, and they are, therefore, in the opinion of a critic, at once competent and severe, worthy to be collected and preserved. Severe is perhaps hardly an epithet ever properly applicable to Mr. Arnold; but his judgment was as serene and unbiassed in regard to his own compositions as in regard to those of any author whom from time to time he criticised. But it was further characteristic of him to be content to say one thing at one time; and he has been accused, not perhaps entirely without reason, of repeating the same thing in the same words, sometimes almost to the weariness of the reader. This habit, however, had at least the effect of fixing in the mind the phrases, and therefore the thoughts or ideas which the phrases conveyed, and with which for the moment he was concerned. But in order to gather the mind of Mr. Arnold on the whole of any subject, literary, political, or religious, it is often necessary to read more than one paper, because in each paper he frequently deals with one aspect of a subject only, which requires, for sound and complete judgment, to be supplemented or completed by another. It is especially necessary to bear this in mind in reading what has become his last utterance on Shelley. In Shelley's case he is known to have intended to write something more; not, indeed, to alter or to qualify what he said, but to say something else which he thought also true, and which needed saying.

This is not the place to attempt a character of Mr. Arnold, even as a critic or an essayist. A preface would expand into a volume if it attempted to indicate even the materials for thought on such subjects, handled by Mr. Arnold, as Poetry, Gray, Keats, Shelley, Byron, Wordsworth (to name no others), which are the subjects of some of the Essays here collected. This is the last volume he ever put together, and it contains some of his ripest, best, most interesting writing.

Perhaps it is well to add that these few words are contributed at the request of others. *Inane munus* indeed, but all that a friend can do!

C.

CONTENTS

THE STUDY OF POETRY[1]

'THE future of poetry is immense, because in poetry, where it is worthy of its high destinies, our race, as time goes on, will find an ever surer and surer stay. There is not a creed which is not shaken, not an accredited dogma which is not shown to be questionable, not a received tradition which does not threaten to dissolve. Our religion has materialised itself in the fact, in the supposed fact; it has attached its emotion to the fact, and now the fact is failing it. But for poetry the idea is everything; the rest is a world of illusion, of divine illusion. Poetry attaches its emotion to

[1] Published in 1880 as the General Introduction to *The English Poets*, edited by T. H. Ward.

the idea.; the idea *is* the fact. The strongest part of our religion to-day is its unconscious poetry.'

Let me be permitted to quote these words of my own, as uttering the thought which should, in my opinion, go with us and govern us in all our study of poetry. In the present work it is the course of one great contributory stream to the world-river of poetry that we are invited to follow. We are here invited to trace the stream of English poetry. But whether we set ourselves, as here, to follow only one of the several streams that make the mighty river of poetry, or whether we seek to know them all, our governing thought should be the same. We should conceive of poetry worthily, and more highly than it has been the custom to conceive of it. We should conceive of it as capable of higher uses, and called to higher destinies, than those which in general men have assigned to it hitherto. More and more mankind will discover that we have to turn to poetry to interpret life for us, to console us, to sustain us. Without poetry, our science will appear incomplete ; and most of what now passes with us for religion and philosophy will be replaced by poetry. Science, I say, will appear incomplete without it. For finely and truly does Wordsworth call poetry 'the impassioned expression which is in the countenance of all science'; and what is a countenance without its expression? Again, Wordsworth finely and truly calls poetry 'the breath and finer spirit of all knowledge': our religion, parading evidences such as those on which the popular mind relies now; our philosophy, pluming itself on its reasonings about causation and finite and infinite being; what are they but the shadows and dreams and false shows of knowledge? The day will come when we shall wonder at ourselves for having trusted to them, for having taken them seriously; and the more we perceive their hollowness, the more we shall prize 'the breath and finer spirit of knowledge' offered to us by poetry.

But if we conceive thus highly of the destinies of poetry, we must also set our standard for poetry high, since poetry, to be capable of fulfilling such high destinies, must be poetry of a high order of excellence. We must accustom ourselves to a high standard and to a strict judgment. Sainte-Beuve relates that Napoleon one day said, when somebody was spoken of in his presence as a charlatan : 'Charlatan as much as you please ; but where is there *not* charlatanism ?'—'Yes,' answers Sainte-Beuve, 'in politics, in the art of governing mankind, that is perhaps true. But in the order of thought, in art, the glory, the eternal honour is that charlatanism shall find no entrance ; herein lies the inviolableness of that noble portion of man's being.' It is admirably said, and let us hold fast to it. In poetry, which is thought and art in one, it is the glory, the eternal honour, that charlatanism shall find no entrance ; that this noble sphere be kept inviolate and inviolable. Charlatanism is for confusing or obliterating the distinctions between excellent and inferior, sound and unsound or only half-sound, true and untrue or only half-true. It is charlatanism, conscious or unconscious, whenever we confuse or obliterate these. And in poetry, more than anywhere else, it is unpermissible to confuse or obliterate them. For in poetry the distinction between excellent and inferior, sound and unsound or only half-sound, true and untrue or only half-true, is of paramount importance. It is of paramount importance because of the high destinies of poetry. In poetry, as a criticism of life under the conditions fixed for such a criticism by the laws of poetic truth and poetic beauty, the spirit of our race will find, we have said, as time. goes on and as other helps fail, its consolation and stay. But the consolation and stay will be of power in proportion to the power of the criticism of life. And the criticism of life will be of power in proportion as the poetry conveying it is excellent rather than inferior, sound rather than unsound or half-sound, true rather than untrue or half-true.

The best poetry is what we want; the best poetry will be found to have a power of forming, sustaining, and delighting us, as nothing else can. A clearer, deeper sense of the best in poetry, and of the strength and joy to be drawn from it, is the most precious benefit which we can gather from a poetical collection such as the present. And yet in the very nature and conduct of such a collection there is inevitably something which tends to obscure in us the consciousness of what our benefit should be, and to distract us from the pursuit of it. We should therefore steadily set it before our minds at the outset, and should compel ourselves to revert constantly to the thought of it as we proceed.

Yes ; constantly in reading poetry, a sense for the best, the really excellent, and of the strength and joy to be drawn from it, should be present in our minds and should govern our estimate of what we read. But this real estimate, the only true one, is liable to be superseded, if we are not watchful, by two other kinds of estimate, the historic estimate and the personal estimate, both of which are fallacious. A poet or a poem may count to us historically, they may count to us on grounds personal to ourselves, and they may count to us really. They may count to us historically. The course of development of a nation's language, thought, and poetry, is profoundly interesting; and by regarding a poet's work as a stage in this course of development we may easily bring ourselves to make it of more importance as poetry than in itself it really is, we may come to use a language of quite exaggerated praise in criticising it; in short, to over-rate it. So arises in our poetic judgments the fallacy caused by the estimate which we may call historic. Then, again, a poet or a poem may count to us on grounds personal to ourselves. Our personal affinities, likings, and circumstances, have great power to sway our estimate of this or that poet's work, and to make us attach more importance to it as poetry than in itself it really possesses, because to us it is, or has been, of high importance. Here also we over-rate the object of our interest, and apply to it a language of praise which is quite exaggerated. And thus we get the source of a second fallacy in our poetic judgments—the fallacy caused by an estimate which we may call personal.

Both fallacies are natural. It is evident how naturally the study of the history and development of a poetry may incline a man to pause over reputations and works once conspicuous but now obscure, and to quarrel with a careless public for skipping, in obedience to mere tradition and habit, from one famous name or work in its national poetry to another, ignorant of what it misses, and of the reason for keeping what it keeps, and of the whole process of growth in its poetry. The French have become diligent students of their own early poetry, which they long neglected; the study makes many of them dissatisfied with their so-called classical poetry, the court-tragedy of the seventeenth century, a poetry which Pellisson long ago reproached with its want of the true poetic stamp, with its *politesse stérile et rampante*, but which nevertheless has reigned in France as absolutely as if it had been the perfection of classical poetry indeed. The dissatisfaction is natural; yet a lively and accomplished critic, M. Charles d'Héricault, the editor of Clément Marot, goes too far when he says that 'the cloud of glory playing round a classic is a mist as dangerous to the future of a literature as it is intolerable for the purposes of history.' 'It hinders,' he goes on, 'it hinders us from seeing more than one single point, the culminating and exceptional point; the summary, fictitious and arbitrary, of a thought and of a work. It substitutes a halo for a physiognomy, it puts a statue where there was once a man, and hiding from us all trace of the labour, the attempts, the weaknesses, the failures, it claims not study but veneration; it does not show us how the thing is done, it imposes upon us a model. Above all, for the historian this creation of classic personages is inadmissible; for it withdraws the poet from his time, from his proper life, it breaks historical relationships, it blinds criticism by conventional admiration, and renders the investigation of literary origins unacceptable. It gives us a human personage no longer, but a God seated immovable amidst His perfect work, like Jupiter on Olympus; and hardly will it be

possible for the young student, to whom such
work is exhibited at such a distance from him, to
believe that it did not issue ready made from that
divine head.'

All this is brilliantly and tellingly said, but we
must plead for a distinction. Everything depends
on the reality of a poet's classic character. If he
is a dubious classic, let us sift him ; if he is a
false classic, let us explode him. But if he is a
real classic, if his work belongs to the class of the
very best (for this is the true and right meaning of
the word *classic, classical*), then the great thing for
us is to feel and enjoy his work as deeply as ever
we can, and to appreciate the wide difference between it and all work which has not the same
high character. This is what is salutary, this is
what is formative ; this is the great benefit to be
got from the study of poetry. Everything which
interferes with it, which hinders it, is injurious.
True, we must read our classic with open eyes, and
not with eyes blinded with superstition ; we must
perceive when his work comes short, when it

drops out of the class of the very best, and we
must rate it, in such cases, at its proper value.
But the use of this negative criticism is not in
itself, it is entirely in its enabling us to have a
clearer sense and a deeper enjoyment of what is
truly excellent. To trace the labour, the attempts,
the weaknesses, the failures of a genuine classic,
to acquaint oneself with his time and his life and
his historical relationships, is mere literary dilet-
tantism unless it has that clear sense and deeper
enjoyment for its end. It may be said that the
more we know about a classic the better we shall
enjoy him ; and, if we lived as long as Methuselah
and had all of us heads of perfect clearness and
wills of perfect steadfastness, this might be true
in fact as it is plausible in theory. But the case
here is much the same as the case with the Greek
and Latin studies of our schoolboys. The elaborate
philological groundwork which we require them
to lay is in theory an admirable preparation for
appreciating the Greek and Latin authors worthily.
The more thoroughly we lay the groundwork, the

better we shall be able, it may be said, to enjoy the authors. True, if time were not so short, and schoolboys' wits not so soon tired and their power of attention exhausted ; only, as it is, the elaborate philological preparation goes on, but the authors are little known and less enjoyed. So with the investigator of 'historic origins' in poetry. He ought to enjoy the true classic all the better for his investigations; he often is distracted from the enjoyment of the best, and with the less good he overbusies himself, and is prone to over-rate it in proportion to the trouble which it has cost him.

The idea of tracing historic origins and historical relationships cannot be absent from a compilation like the present. And naturally the poets to be exhibited in it will be assigned to those persons for exhibition who are known to prize them highly, rather than to those who have no special inclination towards them. Moreover the very occupation with an author, and the business of exhibiting him, disposes us to affirm and amplify his importance. In the present work.

therefore, we are sure of frequent temptation to
adopt the historic estimate, or the personal estimate, and to forget the real estimate; which
latter, nevertheless, we must employ if we are to
make poetry yield us its full benefit. So high is
that benefit, the benefit of clearly feeling and of
deeply enjoying the really excellent, the truly
classic in poetry, that we do well, I say, to set it
fixedly before our minds as our object in studying
poets and poetry, and to make the desire of at-
taining it the one principle to which, as the
Imitation says, whatever we may read or come to
know, we always return. *Cum multa legeris et cog-
noveris, ad unum semper oportet redire principium.*

The historic estimate is likely in especial to
affect our judgment and our language when we
are dealing with ancient poets; the personal
estimate when we are dealing with poets our contemporaries, or at any rate modern. The exaggerations due to the historic estimate are not in
themselves, perhaps, of very much gravity. Their
report hardly enters the general ear; probably

they do not always impose even on the literary men who adopt them. But they lead to a dangerous abuse of language. So we hear Cædmon, amongst our own poets, compared to Milton. I have already noticed the enthusiasm of one accomplished French critic for 'historic origins.' Another eminent French critic, M. Vitet, comments upon that famous document of the early poetry of his nation, the *Chanson de Roland*. It is indeed a most interesting document. The *joculator* or *jongleur* Taillefer, who was with William the Conqueror's army at Hastings, marched before the Norman troops, so said the tradition, singing ' of Charlemagne and of Roland and of Oliver, and of the vassals who died at Roncevaux' ; and it is suggested that in the *Chanson de Roland* by one Turoldus or Théroulde, a poem preserved in a manuscript of the twelfth century in the Bodleian Library at Oxford. we have certainly the matter, perhaps even some of the words, of the chant which Taillefer sang. The poem has vigour and freshness ; it is not without pathos. But M.

Vitet is not satisfied with seeing in it a document
of some poetic value, and of very high historic
and linguistic value; he sees in it a grand and
beautiful work, a monument of epic genius. In its
general design he finds the grandiose conception,
in its details he finds the constant union of simplicity with greatness, which are the marks, he
truly says, of the genuine epic, and distinguish
it from the artificial epic of literary ages. One
thinks of Homer; this is the sort of praise which
is given to Homer, and justly given. Higher
praise there cannot well be, and it is the praise
due to epic poetry of the highest order only, and
to no other. Let us try, then, the *Chanson de
Roland* at its best. Roland, mortally wounded,
lays himself down under a pine-tree, with his face
turned towards Spain and the enemy—

> ' De plusurs choses à remembrer li prist,
> De tantes teres cume li bers cunquist,
> De dulce France, des humes de sun lign,
> De Carlemagne sun seignor ki l'nurrit.'[1]

---

[1] 'Then began he to call many things to remembrance,—all
the lands which his valour conquered, and pleasant France.

That is primitive work, I repeat, with an undeniable poetic quality of its own. It deserves such praise, and such praise is sufficient for it. But now turn to Homer—

Ὥς φάτο· τοὺς δ ἤδη κατέχεν φυσίζοος αἶα
ἐν Λακεδαίμονι αὖθι, φίλῃ ἐν πατρίδι γαίῃ.[1]

We are here in another world, another order of poetry altogether; here is rightly due such supreme praise as that which M. Vitet gives to the *Chanson de Roland*. If our words are to have any meaning, if our judgments are to have any solidity, we must not heap that supreme praise upon poetry of an order immeasurably inferior.

Indeed there can be no more useful help for discovering what poetry belongs to the class of the truly excellent, and can therefore do us most good, than to have always in one's mind lines and

and the men of his lineage, and Charlemagne his liege lord who nourished him.'—*Chanson de Roland*, iii. 939-942.

[1] So said she; they long since in Earth's soft arms were reposing,
There, in their own dear land, their fatherland, Lacedæmon.'
Iliad, iii. 243, 244 (translated by Dr. Hawtrey).

expressions of the great masters, and to apply them as a touchstone to other poetry. Of course we are not to require this other poetry to resemble them ; it may be very dissimilar. But if we have any tact we shall find them, when we have lodged them well in our minds, an infallible touchstone for detecting the presence or absence of high poetic quality, and also the degree of this quality, in all other poetry which we may place beside them. Short passages, even single lines, will serve our turn quite sufficiently. Take the two lines which I have just quoted from Homer, the poet's comment on Helen's mention of her brothers ; —or take his

Ἀ δειλώ, τί σφῶϊ δόμεν Πηλῆϊ ἄνακτι
θνητῷ ; ὑμεῖς δ' ἐστὸν ἀγήρω τ' ἀθανάτω τε.
ἦ ἵνα δυστήνοισι μετ' ἀνδράσιν ἄλγε' ἔχητον ;[1]

the address of Zeus to the horses of Peleus ;—or take finally his

---

[1] 'Ah, unhappy pair, why gave we you to King Peleus, to a mortal ? but ye are without old age, and immortal. Was it that with men born to misery ye might have sorrow !'—*Iliad*, xvii. 443-445.

C

Καὶ σέ, γέρον, τὸ πρὶν μὲν ἀκούομεν ὄλβιον εἶναι·[1]

the words of Achilles to Priam, a suppliant before him. Take that incomparable line and a half of Dante, Ugolino's tremendous words—

> ' Io no piangeva ; sì dentro impietrai.
> Piangevan elli . . .'[2]

take the lovely words of Beatrice to Virgil—

> ' Io son fatta da Dio, sua mercè, tale,
> Che la vostra miseria non mi tange,
> Nè fiamma d'esto incendio non m'assale . . .'[3]

take the simple, but perfect, single line—

> ' In la sua volontade è nostra pace.'[4]

Take of Shakespeare a line or two of Henry the Fourth's expostulation with sleep—

> ' Wilt thou upon the high and giddy mast
> Seal up the ship-boy's eyes, and rock his brains
> In cradle of the rude imperious surge . . .'

---

[1] 'Nay, and thou too, old man, in former days wast, as we hear, happy.'—*Iliad*, xxiv. 543.

[2] ' I wailed not, so of stone grew I within ;—*they* wailed.'— *Inferno*, xxxiii. 39, 40.

[3] ' Of such sort hath God, thanked be His mercy, made me, that your misery toucheth me not, neither doth the flame of this fire strike me.'—*Inferno*, ii. 91-93.

[4] ' In His will is our peace.'—*Paradiso*, iii. 85.

and take, as well, Hamlet's dying request to
Horatio—

> 'If thou didst ever hold me in thy heart,
>   Absent thee from felicity awhile,
>   And in this harsh world draw thy breath in pain
>   To tell my story . . .'

Take of Milton that Miltonic passage—

>   'Darken'd so, yet shone
>   Above them all the archangel ; but his face
>   Deep scars of thunder had intrench'd, and care
>   Sat on his faded cheek . . .'

add two such lines as—

> 'And courage never to submit or yield
>   And what is else not to be overcome . . .'

and finish with the exquisite close to the loss of
Proserpine, the loss

>   '. . . which cost Ceres all that pain
>   To seek her through the world.'

These few lines, if we have tact and can use them,
are enough even of themselves to keep clear and
sound our judgments about poetry, to save us from
fallacious estimates of it, to conduct us to a real
estimate.

The specimens I have quoted differ widely from one another, but they have in common this: the possession of the very highest poetical quality. If we are thoroughly penetrated by their power, we shall find that we have acquired a sense enabling us, whatever poetry may be laid before us, to feel the degree in which a high poetical quality is present or wanting there. Critics give themselves great labour to draw out what in the abstract constitutes the characters of a high quality of poetry. It is much better simply to have recourse to concrete examples ;—to take specimens of poetry of the high, the very highest quality, and to say : The characters of a high quality of poetry are what is expressed *there*. They are far better recognised by being felt in the verse of the master, than by being perused in the prose of the critic. Nevertheless if we are urgently pressed to give some critical account of them, we may safely, perhaps, venture on laying down, not indeed how and why the characters arise, but where and in what they arise. They are in the matter and substance of the poetry, and they are in its manner and style. Both of these, the substance and matter on the one hand, the style and manner on the other, have a mark, an accent, of high beauty, worth, and power. But if we are asked to define this mark and accent in the abstract, our answer must be : No, for we should thereby be darkening the question, not clearing it. The mark and accent are as given by the substance and matter of that poetry, by the style and manner of that poetry, and of all other poetry which is akin to it in quality.

Only one thing we may add as to the substance and matter of poetry, guiding ourselves by Aristotle's profound observation that the superiority of poetry over history consists in its possessing a higher truth and a higher seriousness (φιλοσο-φώτερον καὶ σπουδαιότερον). Let us add, there-fore, to what we have said, this : that the substance and matter of the best poetry acquire their special character from possessing, in an eminent degree, truth and seriousness. We may add yet further, what is in itself evident, that to the style and manner of the best poetry their special character, their accent, is given by their diction, and, even yet more, by their movement. And though we distinguish between the two characters, the two accents, of superiority, yet they are nevertheless vitally connected one with the other. The superior character of truth and seriousness, in the matter and substance of the best poetry, is inseparable from the superiority of diction and movement marking its style and manner. The two superiorities are closely related, and are in steadfast proportion one to the other. So far as high poetic truth and seriousness are wanting to a poet's matter and substance, so far also, we may be sure, will a high poetic stamp of diction and movement be wanting to his style and manner. In proportion as this high stamp of diction and movement, again, is absent from a poet's style and manner, we shall find, also, that high poetic truth and seriousness are absent from his substance and matter.

So stated, these are but dry generalities; their whole force lies in their application. And I could wish every student of poetry to make the application of them for himself. Made by himself, the application would impress itself upon his mind far more deeply than made by me. Neither will my limits allow me to make any full application of the generalities above propounded; but in the hope of bringing out, at any rate, some significance in them, and of establishing an important principle more firmly by their means, I will, in the space which remains to me, follow rapidly from the commencement the course of our English poetry with them in my view.

Once more I return to the early poetry of France, with which our own poetry, in its origins, is indissolubly connected. In the twelfth and thirteenth centuries, that seed-time of all modern language and literature, the poetry of France had a clear predominance in Europe. Of the two divisions of that poetry, its productions in the *langue d'oil* and its productions in the *langue d'oc,* the poetry of the *langue d'oc*, of southern France, of the troubadours, is of importance because of its effect on Italian literature ;—the first literature of modern Europe to strike the true and grand note, and to bring forth, as in Dante and Petrarch it brought forth, classics. But the predominance of French poetry in Europe, during the twelfth and thirteenth centuries, is due to its poetry of the *langue d'oil*, the poetry of northern France and of the tongue which is now the French language. In the twelfth century the bloom of this romance-poetry was earlier and stronger in England, at the court of our Anglo-Norman kings, than in France itself. But it was a bloom of French poetry ; and as our native poetry formed itself, it formed itself out of this. The romance-poems which took possession of the heart and imagination of Europe in the twelfth and thirteenth centuries are French ; 'they are,' as Southey justly says, 'the pride of French literature, nor have we anything which can be placed in competition with them.' Themes were supplied from all quarters ; but the romance-

setting which was common to them all, and which
gained the ear of Europe, was French.   This con-
stituted for the French poetry, literature, and language, at the height of the Middle Age, an un-
challenged predominance.   The Italian Brunetto
Latini, the master of Dante, wrote his *Treasure* in
French because, he says, 'la parleure en est plus
délitable et plus commune à toutes gens.'   In the
same century, the thirteenth, the French romance-
writer, Christian of Troyes, formulates the claims,
in chivalry and letters, of France, his native
country, as follows :—

> ' Or vous ert par ce livre apris,
>   Que Gresse ot de chevalerie
>   Le premier los et de clergie ;
>   Puis vint chevalerie à Rome,
>   Et de la clergie la some,
>   Qui ore est en France venue.
>   Diex doinst qu'ele i soit retenue,
>   Et que li lius li abelisse
>   Tant que de France n'isse
>   L'onor qui s'i est arestée ! '

'Now by this book you will learn that first
Greece had the renown for chivalry and letters ;

then chivalry and the primacy in letters passed
to Rome, and now it is come to France. God
grant it may be kept there; and that the place
may please it so well, that the honour which has
come to make stay in France may never depart
thence!'

Yet it is now all gone, this French romance-
poetry, of which the weight of substance and the
power of style are not unfairly represented by
this extract from Christian of Troyes. Only by
means of the historic estimate can we persuade
ourselves now to think that any of it is of poetical
importance.

But in the fourteenth century there comes an
Englishman nourished on this poetry, taught his
trade by this poetry, getting words, rhyme, metre
from this poetry; for even of that stanza which
the Italians used, and which Chaucer derived
immediately from the Italians, the basis and sug-
gestion was probably given in France. Chaucer
(I have already named him) fascinated his contemporaries, but so too did Christian of Troyes

and Wolfram of Eschenbach. Chaucer's power of fascination, however, is enduring; his poetical importance does not need the assistance of the historic estimate; it is real. He is a genuine source of joy and strength, which is flowing still for us and will flow always. He will be read, as time goes on, far more generally than he is read now. His language is a cause of difficulty for us; but so also, and I think in quite as great a degree, is the language of Burns. In Chaucer's case, as in that of Burns, it is a difficulty to be unhesitatingly accepted and overcome.

If we ask ourselves wherein consists the immense superiority of Chaucer's poetry over the romance-poetry—why it is that in passing from this to Chaucer we suddenly feel ourselves to be in another world, we shall find that his superiority is both in the substance of his poetry and in the style of his poetry. His superiority in substance is given by his large, free, simple, clear yet kindly view of human life,—so unlike the total want, in the romance-poets, of all intelligent command of it. Chaucer has not their helplessness; he has gained the power to survey the world from a central, a truly human point of view. We have only to call to mind the Prologue to *The Canterbury Tales*. The right comment upon it is Dryden's: 'It is sufficient to say, according to the proverb, that *here is God's plenty*.' And again: 'He is a perpetual fountain of good sense.' It is by a large, free, sound representation of things, that poetry, this high criticism of life, has truth of substance; and Chaucer's poetry has truth of substance.

Of his style and manner, if we think first of the romance-poetry and then of Chaucer's divine liquidness of diction, his divine fluidity of movement, it is difficult to speak temperately. They are irresistible, and justify all the rapture with which his successors speak of his 'gold dew-drops of speech.' Johnson misses the point entirely when he finds fault with Dryden for ascribing to Chaucer the first refinement of our numbers, and says that Gower also can show smooth numbers and easy rhymes. The refinement of our numbers

means something far more than this. A nation
may have versifiers with smooth numbers and
easy rhymes, and yet may have no real poetry at
all. Chaucer is the father of our splendid English
poetry ; he is our 'well of English undefiled,'
because by the lovely charm of his diction, the
lovely charm of his movement, he makes an
epoch and founds a tradition. In Spenser, Shakespeare, Milton, Keats, we can follow the tradition of the liquid diction, the fluid movement, of
Chaucer ; at one time it is his liquid diction of
which in these poets we feel the virtue, and at
another time it is his fluid movement. And the
virtue is irresistible.

Bounded as is my space, I must yet find room
for an example of Chaucer's virtue, as I have
given examples to show the virtue of the great
classics. I feel disposed to say that a single line
is enough to show the charm of Chaucer's verse ;
that merely one line like this—

              'O martyr souded[1] in virginitee !'

---

[1] The French *soudé ;* soldered, fixed fast.

has a virtue of manner and movement such as we
shall not find in all the verse of romance-poetry ;
—but this is saying nothing. The virtue is such
as we shall not find, perhaps, in all English
poetry, outside the poets whom I have named as
the special inheritors of Chaucer's tradition. A
single line, however, is too little if we have not the
strain of Chaucer's verse well in our memory; let us
take a stanza. It is from *The Prioress's Tale*, the
story of the Christian child murdered in a Jewry—

> ' My throte is cut unto my nekke-bone
> Saidè this child, and as by way of kinde
> I should have deyd, yea, longè time agone ;
> But Jesu Christ, as ye in bookès finde,
> Will that his glory last and be in minde,
> And for the worship of his mother dere
> Yet may I sing *O Alma* loud and clere.'

Wordsworth has modernised this Tale, and to feel
how delicate and evanescent is the charm of verse,
we have only to read Wordsworth's first three
lines of this stanza after Chaucer's—

> ' My throat is cut unto the bone, I trow,
> Said this young child, and by the law of kind
> I should have died, yea, many hours ago.'

The charm is departed. It is often said that the power of liquidness and fluidity in Chaucer's verse was dependent upon a free, a licentious dealing with language, such as is now impossible; upon a liberty, such as Burns too enjoyed, of making words like *neck, bird*, into a dissyllable by adding to them, and words like *cause, rhyme*, into a dissyllable by sounding the *e* mute. It is true that Chaucer's fluidity is conjoined with this liberty, and is admirably served by it ; but we ought not to say that it was dependent upon it. It was dependent upon his talent. Other poets with a like liberty do not attain to the fluidity of Chaucer ; Burns himself does not attain to it. Poets, again, who have a talent akin to Chaucer's, such as Shakespeare or Keats, have known how to attain to his fluidity without the like liberty.

And yet Chaucer is not one of the great classics. His poetry transcends and effaces, easily and without effort, all the romance - poetry of Catholic Christendom ; it transcends and effaces all the English poetry contemporary with it, it transcends and effaces all the English poetry subsequent to it down to the age of Elizabeth. Of such avail is poetic truth of substance, in its natural and necessary union with poetic truth of style. And yet, I say, Chaucer is not one of the great classics. He has not their accent. What is wanting to him is suggested by the mere mention of the name of the first great classic of Christendom, the immortal poet who died eighty years before Chaucer,— Dante. The accent of such verse as

'In la sua volontade è nostra pace . . .'

is altogether beyond Chaucer's reach; we praise him, but we feel that this accent is out of the question for him. It may be said that it was necessarily out of the reach of any poet in the England of that stage of growth. Possibly; but we are to adopt a real, not a historic, estimate of poetry. However we may account for its absence, something is wanting, then, to the poetry of Chaucer, which poetry must have before it can be placed in the glorious class of the best. And there is no doubt what that something is. It is

the σπουδαιότης, the high and excellent seriousness, which Aristotle assigns as one of the grand
virtues of poetry. The substance of Chaucer's
poetry, his view of things and his criticism of life,
has largeness, freedom, shrewdness, benignity; but
it has not this high seriousness. Homer's criticism
of life has it, Dante's has it, Shakespeare's has it.
It is this chiefly which gives to our spirits what
they can rest upon; and with the increasing demands of our modern ages upon poetry, this virtue
of giving us what we can rest upon will be more
and more highly esteemed. A voice from the
slums of Paris, fifty or sixty years after Chaucer,
the voice of poor Villon out of his life of riot and
crime, has at its happy moments (as, for instance,
in the last stanza of *La Belle Heaulmière*[1]) more

---

[1] The name *Heaulmière* is said to be derived from a head-
dress (helm) worn as a mark by courtesans.   In Villon's ballad,
a poor old creature of this class laments her days of youth and
beauty.   The last stanza of the ballad runs thus—

> ' Ainsi le bon temps regretons
> Entre nous, pauvres vieilles sottes,
> Assises bas, à croppetons,
> Tout en ung tas comme pelottes ;
> A petit feu de chenevottes
> Tost allumées, tost estainctes.

of this important poetic virtue of seriousness than all the productions of Chaucer. But its apparition in Villon, and in men like Villon, is fitful; the greatness of the great poets, the power of their criticism of life, is that their virtue is sustained.

To our praise, therefore, of Chaucer as a poet there must be this limitation; he lacks the high seriousness of the great classics, and therewith an important part of their virtue. Still, the main fact for us to bear in mind about Chaucer is his sterling value according to that real estimate which we firmly adopt for all poets. He has poetic truth of substance, though he has not high poetic seriousness, and corresponding to his truth of substance he has an exquisite virtue of style and manner. With him is born our real poetry.

For my present purpose I need not dwell on

> Et jadis fusmes si mignottes !
> Ainsi en prend à maintz et maintes.'

'Thus amongst ourselves we regret the good time, poor silly old things, low-seated on our heels, all in a heap like so many balls ; by a little fire of hemp-stalks, soon lighted, soon spent. And once we were such darlings ! So fares it with many and many a one.'

our Elizabethan poetry, or on the continuation and close of this poetry in Milton. We all of us profess to be agreed in the estimate of this poetry; we all of us recognise it as great poetry, our greatest, and Shakespeare and Milton as our poetical classics. The real estimate, here, has universal currency. With the next age of our poetry divergency and difficulty begin. An historic estimate of that poetry has established itself; and the question is, whether it will be found to coincide with the real estimate.

The age of Dryden, together with our whole eighteenth century which followed it, sincerely believed itself to have produced poetical classics of its own, and even to have made advance, in poetry, beyond all its predecessors. Dryden regards as not seriously disputable the opinion 'that the sweetness of English verse was never understood or practised by our fathers.' Cowley could see nothing at all in Chaucer's poetry. Dryden heartily admired it, and, as we have seen, praised its matter admirably; but of its exquisite manner and movement all he can find to say is that 'there is the rude sweetness of a Scotch tune in it, which is natural and pleasing, though not perfect.' Addison, wishing to praise Chaucer's numbers, compares them with Dryden's own. And all through the eighteenth century, and down even into our own times, the stereotyped phrase of approbation for good verse found in our early poetry has been, that it even approached the verse of Dryden, Addison, Pope, and Johnson.

Are Dryden and Pope poetical classics? Is the historic estimate, which represents them as such, and which has been so long established that it cannot easily give way, the real estimate? Wordsworth and Coleridge, as is well known, denied it; but the authority of Wordsworth and Coleridge does not weigh much with the young generation, and there are many signs to show that the eighteenth century and its judgments are coming into favour again. Are the favourite poets of the eighteenth century classics?

It is impossible within my present limits to

discuss the question fully. And what man of letters would not shrink from seeming to dispose dictatorially of the claims of two men who are, at any rate, such masters in letters as Dryden and Pope ; two men of such admirable talent, both of them, and one of them, Dryden, a man, on all sides, of such energetic and genial power ? And yet, if we are to gain the full benefit from poetry, we must have the real estimate of it. I cast about for some mode of arriving, in the present case, at such an estimate without offence. And perhaps the best way is to begin, as it is easy to begin, with cordial praise.

When we find Chapman, the Elizabethan translator of Homer, expressing himself in his preface thus : 'Though truth in her very nakedness sits in so deep a pit, that from Gades to Aurora and Ganges few eyes can sound her, I hope yet those few here will so discover and confirm that, the date being out of her darkness in this morning of our poet, he shall now gird his temples with the sun,'—we pronounce that such a prose is intoler-

able. When we find Milton writing: 'And long
it was not after, when I was confirmed in this
opinion, that he, who would not be frustrate of
his hope to write well hereafter in laudable things,
ought himself to be a true poem,'—we pronounce
that such a prose has its own grandeur, but that
it is obsolete and inconvenient. But when we
find Dryden telling us : 'What Virgil wrote in
the vigour of his age, in plenty and at ease, I have
undertaken to translate in my declining years ;
struggling with wants, oppressed with sickness,
curbed in my genius, liable to be misconstrued in
all I write,'—then we exclaim that here at last we
have the true English prose, a prose such as we
would all gladly use if we only knew how. Yet
Dryden was Milton's contemporary.

But after the Restoration the time had come
when our nation felt the imperious need of a fit
prose. So, too, the time had likewise come when
our nation felt the imperious need of freeing itself
from the absorbing preoccupation which religion
in the Puritan age had exercised. It was im·

possible that this freedom should be brought
about without some negative excess, without some
neglect and impairment of the religious life of
the soul; and the spiritual history of the eighteenth century shows us that the freedom was not
achieved without them.   Still, the freedom was
achieved; the preoccupation, an undoubtedly
baneful and retarding one if it had continued, was
got rid of.   And as with religion amongst us at
that period, so it was also with letters.   A fit
prose was a necessity; but it was impossible that
a fit prose should establish itself amongst us
without some touch of frost to the imaginative life of the soul.   The needful qualities for
a fit prose are regularity, uniformity, precision,
balance.   The men of letters, whose destiny it
may be to bring their nation to the attainment
of a fit prose, must of necessity, whether they
work in prose or in verse, give a predominat-
ing, an almost exclusive attention to the qualities of regularity, uniformity, precision, balance.
But an almost exclusive attention to these

qualities involves some repression and silencing
of poetry.

We are to regard Dryden as the puissant and
glorious founder, Pope as the splendid high priest,
of our age of prose and reason, of our excellent
and indispensable eighteenth century.   For the
purposes of their mission and destiny their poetry,
like their prose, is admirable.   Do you ask me
whether Dryden's verse, take it almost where you
will, is not good ?

> ' A milk-white Hind, immortal and unchanged,
>   Fed on the lawns and in the forest ranged.'

I answer : Admirable for the purposes of the
inaugurator of an age of prose and reason.   Do
you ask me whether Pope's verse, take it almost
where you will, is not good ?

> ' To Hounslow Heath I point, and Banstead Down ;
>   Thence comes your mutton, and these chicks my own.'

I answer : Admirable for the purposes of the high
priest of an age of prose and reason.   But do you
ask me whether such verse proceeds from men

with an adequate poetic criticism of life, from
men whose criticism of life has a high seriousness,
or even, without that high seriousness, has poetic
largeness, freedom, insight, benignity? Do you
ask me whether the application of ideas to life in
the verse of these men, often a powerful application, no doubt, is a powerful *poetic* application?
Do you ask me whether the poetry of these men
has either the matter or the inseparable manner
of such an adequate poetic criticism; whether it
has the accent of

'Absent thee from felicity awhile . .'
or of

'And what is else not to be overcome . . .'
or of

'O martyr souded in virginitee!'

I answer: It has not and cannot have them; it
is the poetry of the builders of an age of prose
and reason. Though they may write in verse,
though they may in a certain sense be masters of
the art of versification, Dryden and Pope are not

classics of our poetry, they are classics of our prose.

Gray is our poetical classic of that literature and age; the position of Gray is singular, and demands a word of notice here.   He has not the volume or the power of poets who, coming in times more favourable, have attained to an independent criticism of life.   But he lived with the great poets, he lived, above all, with the Greeks, through perpetually studying and enjoying them ; and he caught their poetic point of view for regarding life, caught their poetic manner.   The point of view and the manner are not self-sprung in him, he caught them of others ; and he had not the free and abundant use of them.   But whereas Addison and Pope never had the use of them, Gray had the use of them at times.   He is the scantiest and frailest of classics in our poetry, but he is a classic.

And now, after Gray, we are met, as we draw towards the end of the eighteenth century, we are met by the great name of Burns.   We enter now on times where the personal estimate of poets begins to be rife, and where the real estimate of them is not reached without difficulty. But in spite of the disturbing pressures of personal partiality, of national partiality, let us try to reach a real estimate of the poetry of Burns.

By his English poetry Burns in general belongs to the eighteenth century, and has little importance for us.

'Mark ruffian Violence, distain'd with crimes,
Rousing elate in these degenerate times ;
View unsuspecting Innocence a prey,
As guileful Fraud points out the erring way ;
While subtle Litigation's pliant tongue
The life-blood equal sucks of Right and Wrong !'

Evidently this is not the real Burns, or his name and fame would have disappeared long ago. Nor is Clarinda's love-poet, Sylvander, the real Burns either. But he tells us himself : 'These English songs gravel me to death. I have not the command of the language that I have of my native tongue. In fact, I think that my ideas are more barren in English than in Scotch. I have been at *Duncan Gray* to dress it in English, but all I can do is desperately stupid.' We English turn naturally, in Burns, to the poems in our own language, because we can read them easily ; but in those poems we have not the real Burns.

The real Burns is of course in his Scotch poems. Let us boldly say that of much of this poetry, a poetry dealing perpetually with Scotch drink, Scotch religion, and Scotch manners, a Scotchman's estimate is apt to be personal. A Scotchman is used to this world of Scotch drink, Scotch religion, and Scotch manners ; he has a tenderness for it ; he meets its poet half way. In this tender mood he reads pieces like the *Holy Fair* or *Halloween*. But this world of Scotch drink, Scotch religion, and Scotch manners is against a poet, not for him, when it is not a partial countryman who reads him ; for in itself it is not a beautiful world, and no one can deny that it is of advantage to a poet to deal with a beautiful world. Burns's world of Scotch drink, Scotch religion, and Scotch manners, is often a harsh, a sordid, a repulsive world: even the world of his *Cotter's Saturday Night* is not a beautiful world. No doubt a poet's criticism of life may have such truth and power that it triumphs over its world and delights us. Burns may triumph over his world, often he does triumph over his world, but let us observe how and where. Burns is the first case we have had where the bias of the personal estimate tends to mislead; let us look at him closely, he can bear it.

Many of his admirers will tell us that we have Burns, convivial, genuine, delightful, here—

> ' Leeze me on drink! it gies us mair
>   Than either school or college ;
> It kindles wit, it waukens lair,
>   It pangs us fou o' knowledge.
> Be 't whisky gill or penny wheep
>   Or ony stronger potion,
> It never fails, on drinking deep,
>   To kittle up our notion
>   By night or day.'

There is a great deal of that sort of thing in Burns, and it is unsatisfactory, not because it is bacchanalian poetry, but because it has not that accent of sincerity which bacchanalian poetry, to do it justice, very often has. There is something in it of bravado, something which makes us feel that we have not the man speaking to us with his real voice ; something, therefore, poetically unsound.

With still more confidence will his admirers tell us that we have the genuine Burns, the great poet, when his strain asserts the independence, equality, dignity, of men, as in the famous song *For a' that and a' that*—

> ' A prince can mak' a belted knight,
>   A marquis, duke, and a' that ;
> But an honest man's aboon his might,
>   Guid faith he mauna fa' that !
>   For a' that, and a' that,
>   Their dignities, and a' that,
>   The pith o' sense, and pride o' worth,
>   Are higher rank than a' that.'

Here they find his grand, genuine touches; and still more, when this puissant genius, who so often set morality at defiance, falls moralising—

> ' The sacred lowe o' weel-placed love
>   Luxuriantly indulge it ;
> But never tempt th' illicit rove,
>   Tho' naething should divulge it.

> I waive the quantum o' the sin,
>> The hazard o' concealing,
> But och! it hardens a' within,
>> And petrifies the feeling.'

Or in a higher strain—

> Who made the heart, 'tis He alone
>> Decidedly can try us;
> He knows each chord, its various tone;
>> Each spring, its various bias.
> Then at the balance let's be mute,
>> We never can adjust it;
> What's *done* we partly may compute,
>> But know not what's resisted.'

Or in a better strain yet, a strain, his admirers
will say, unsurpassable—

> ' To make a happy fire-side clime
>> To weans and wife,
> That's the true pathos and sublime
>> Of human life.'

There is criticism of life for you, the admirers of
Burns will say to us; there is the application
of ideas to life! There is, undoubtedly. The
doctrine of the last-quoted lines coincides almost
exactly with what was the aim and end, Xenophon
tells us, of all the teaching of Socrates. And the

application is a powerful one; made by a man of vigorous understanding, and (need I say?) a master of language.

But for supreme poetical success more is required than the powerful application of ideas to life; it must be an application under the conditions fixed by the laws of poetic truth and poetic beauty. Those laws fix as an essential condition, in the poet's treatment of such matters as are here in question, high seriousness;—the high seriousness which comes from absolute sincerity. The accent of high seriousness, born of absolute sincerity, is what gives to such verse as

    'In la sua volontade è nostra pace . . '

to such criticism of life as Dante's, its power. Is this accent felt in the passages which I have been quoting from Burns? Surely not; surely, if our sense is quick, we must perceive that we have not in those passages a voice from the very inmost soul of the genuine Burns; he is not speaking to us from these depths, he is more or less preaching.

And the compensation for admiring such passages less, from missing the perfect poetic accent in them, will be that we shall admire more the poetry where that accent is found.

No; Burns, like Chaucer, comes short of the high seriousness of the great classics, and the virtue of matter and manner which goes with that high seriousness is wanting to his work. At moments he touches it in a profound and passionate melancholy, as in those four immortal lines taken by Byron as a motto for *The Bride of Abydos*, but which have in them a depth of poetic quality such as resides in no verse of Byron's own—

> ' Had we never loved sae kindly,
> Had we never loved sae blindly,
> Never met, or never parted,
> We had ne'er been broken-hearted.'

But a whole poem of that quality Burns cannot make; the rest, in the *Farewell to Nancy*, is verbiage.

We arrive best at the real estimate of Burns, I

think, by conceiving his work as having truth of matter and truth of manner, but not the accent or the poetic virtue of the highest masters. His genuine criticism of life, when the sheer poet in him speaks, is ironic ; it is not—

'Thou Power Supreme, whose mighty scheme
These woes of mine fulfil,
Here firm I rest, they must be best
Because they are Thy will !'

It is far rather : *Whistle owre the lave o't !* Yet we may say of him as of Chaucer, that of life and the world, as they come before him, his view is large, free, shrewd, benignant,—truly poetic, therefore ; and his manner of rendering what he sees is to match. But we must note, at the same time, his great difference from Chaucer. The freedom of Chaucer is heightened, in Burns, by a fiery, reckless energy ; the benignity of Chaucer deepens, in Burns, into an overwhelming sense of the pathos of things ;—of the pathos of human nature, the pathos, also, of non-human nature. Instead of the fluidity of Chaucer's manner, the manner of

Burns has spring, bounding swiftness. Burns is by far the greater force, though he has perhaps less charm. The world of Chaucer is fairer, richer, more significant than that of Burns; but when the largeness and freedom of Burns get full sweep, as in *Tam o' Shanter*, or still more in that puissant and splendid production, *The Jolly Beggars*, his world may be what it will, his poetic genius triumphs over it. In the world of *The Jolly Beggars* there is more than hideousness and squalor, there is bestiality; yet the piece is a superb poetic success. It has a breadth, truth, and power which make the famous scene in Auerbach's Cellar, of Goethe's *Faust*, seem artificial and tame beside it, and which are only matched by Shakespeare and Aristophanes.

Here, where his largeness and freedom serve him so admirably, and also in those poems and songs where to shrewdness he adds infinite archness and wit, and to benignity infinite pathos, where his manner is flawless, and a perfect poetic whole is the result,—in things like the address to the mouse whose home he had ruined, in things like *Duncan Gray, Tam Glen, Whistle and I'll come to you my Lad, Auld Lang Syne* (this list might be made much longer),—here we have the genuine Burns, of whom the real estimate must be high indeed. Not a classic, nor with the excellent σπουδαιότης of the great classics, nor with a verse rising to a criticism of life and a virtue like theirs; but a poet with thorough truth of substance and an answering truth of style, giving us a poetry sound to the core. We all of us have a leaning towards the pathetic, and may be inclined perhaps to prize Burns most for his touches of piercing, sometimes almost intolerable, pathos; for verse like—

> 'We twa hae paidl't i' the burn
>   From mornin' sun till dine;
> But seas between us braid hae roar'd
>   Sin auld lang syne . . .'

where he is as lovely as he is sound. But perhaps it is by the perfection of soundness of his lighter and archer masterpieces that he is poetically most

wholesome for us. For the votary misled by a
personal estimate of Shelley, as so many of us
have been, are, and will be, — of that beautiful
spirit building his many-coloured haze of words
and images

  'Pinnacled dim in the intense inane '—

no contact can be wholesomer than the contact
with Burns at his archest and soundest. Side by
side with the

'On the brink of the night and the morning
    My coursers are wont to respire,
But the Earth has just whispered a warning
    That their flight must be swifter than fire . . .

of *Prometheus Unbound*, how salutary, how very
salutary, to place this from *Tam Glen*—

    'My minnie does constantly deave me
        And bids me beware o' young men ;
    They flatter, she says, to deceive me ;
        But wha can think sae o' Tam Glen ?'

But we enter on burning ground as we approach
the poetry of times so near to us—poetry like that
of Byron, Shelley, and Wordsworth—of which the

estimates are so often not only personal, but personal with passion. For my purpose, it is enough to have taken the single case of Burns, the first poet we come to of whose work the estimate formed is evidently apt to be personal, and to have suggested how we may proceed, using the poetry of the great classics as a sort of touchstone, to correct this estimate, as we had previously corrected by the same means the historic estimate where we met with it. A collection like the present, with its succession of celebrated names and celebrated poems, offers a good opportunity to us for resolutely endeavouring to make our estimates of poetry real. I have sought to point out a method which will help us in making them so, and to exhibit it in use so far as to put any one who likes in a way of applying it for himself.

At any rate the end to which the method and the estimate are designed to lead, and from leading to which, if they do lead to it, they get their whole value,—the benefit of being able clearly to feel and deeply to enjoy the best, the truly classic, in poetry, — is an end, let me say it once more at parting, of supreme importance. We are often told that an era is opening in which we are to see multitudes of a common sort of readers, and masses of a common sort of literature ; that such readers do not want and could not relish anything better than such literature, and that to provide it is becoming a vast and profitable industry. Even if good literature entirely lost currency with the world, it would still be abundantly worth while to continue to enjoy it by oneself. But it never will lose currency with the world, in spite of momentary appearances ; it never will lose supremacy. Currency and supremacy are insured to it, not indeed by the world's deliberate and conscious choice, but by something far deeper,—by the instinct of self-preservation in humanity.

II

MILTON [1]

THE most eloquent voice of our century uttered, shortly before leaving the world, a warning cry against 'the Anglo-Saxon contagion.' The tendencies and aims, the view of life and the social economy of the ever-multiplying and spreading Anglo-Saxon race, would be found congenial, this prophet feared, by all the prose, all the vulgarity amongst mankind, and would invade and overpower all nations. The true ideal would be lost, a general sterility of mind and heart would set in.

The prophet had in view, no doubt, in the warning thus given, us and our colonies, but the

[1] An address delivered in St. Margaret's Church, Westminster, on the 13th of February 1888, at the unveiling of a Memorial Window presented by Mr. George W. Childs of Philadelphia.

United States still more. There the Anglo-Saxon race is already most numerous, there it increases fastest ; there material interests are most absorbing and pursued with most energy ; there the ideal, the saving ideal, of a high and rare excellence, seems perhaps to suffer most danger of being obscured and lost. Whatever one may think of the general danger to the world from the Anglo-Saxon contagion, it appears to me difficult to deny that the growing greatness and influence of the United States does bring with it some danger to the ideal of a high and rare excellence. The *average man* is too much a religion there; his performance is unduly magnified, his shortcomings are not duly seen and admitted. A lady in the State of Ohio sent to me only the other day a volume on American authors ; the praise given throughout was of such high pitch that in thanking her I could not forbear saying that for only one or two of the authors named was such a strain of praise admissible, and that we lost all real standard of excellence by praising so uniformly and immoderately. She answered me with charming good temper, that very likely I was quite right, but it was pleasant to her to think that excellence was common and abundant. But excellence is not common and abundant; on the contrary, as the Greek poet long ago said, excellence dwells among rocks hardly accessible, and a man must almost wear his heart out before he can reach her. Whoever talks of excellence as common and abundant, is on the way to lose all right standard of excellence. And when the right standard of excellence is lost, it is not likely that much which is excellent will be produced.

To habituate ourselves, therefore, to approve, as the Bible says, things that are really excellent, is of the highest importance. And some apprehension may justly be caused by a tendency in Americans to take, or, at any rate, attempt to take, profess to take, the average man and his performances too seriously, to over-rate and over-praise what is not really superior.

But we have met here to-day to witness the unveiling of a gift in Milton's honour, and a gift bestowed by an American, Mr. Childs of Philadelphia; whose cordial hospitality so many Englishmen, I myself among the number, have experienced in America. It was only last autumn that Stratford-upon-Avon celebrated the reception of a gift from the same generous donor in honour of Shakespeare. Shakespeare and Milton——he who wishes to keep his standard of excellence high, cannot choose two better objects of regard and honour. And it is an American who has chosen them, and whose beautiful gift in honour of one of them, Milton, with Mr. Whittier's simple and true lines inscribed upon it, is unveiled to-day. Perhaps this gift in honour of Milton, of which I am asked to speak, is, even more than the gift in honour of Shakespeare, one to suggest edifying reflections to us.

Like Mr. Whittier, I treat the gift of Mr. Childs as a gift in honour of Milton, although the window given is in memory of his second wife, Catherine Woodcock, the 'late espoused saint' of

the famous sonnet, who died in child-bed at the
end of the first year of her marriage with Milton,
and who lies buried here with her infant. Milton
is buried in Cripplegate, but he lived for a good
while in this parish of St. Margaret's, Westminster,
and here he composed part of *Paradise Lost*, and
the whole of *Paradise Regained* and *Samson Agonistes*. When death deprived him of the Catherine
whom the new window commemorates, Milton
had still some eighteen years to live, and Crom-
well, his 'chief of men,' was yet ruling England.
But the Restoration, with its 'Sons of Belial,' was
not far off; and in the meantime Milton's heavy
affliction had laid fast hold upon him, his eyesight
had failed totally; he was blind. In what remained to him of life he had the consolation of
producing the *Paradise Lost* and the *Samson
Agonistes*, and such a consolation we may indeed
count as no slight one. But the daily life of happiness in common things and in domestic affections—a life of which, to Milton as to Dante, too
small a share was given—he seems to have known

most, if not only, in his one married year with
the wife who is here buried.   Her form 'vested all
in white,' as in his sonnet he relates that after her
death she appeared to him, her face veiled, but
with 'love, sweetness, and goodness' shining in her
person,—this fair and gentle daughter of the rigid
sectarist of Hackney, this lovable companion with
whom Milton had rest and happiness one year, is
a part of Milton indeed, and in calling up her
memory, we call up his.

And in calling up Milton's memory we call up,
let me say, a memory upon which, in prospect of
the Anglo-Saxon contagion and of its dangers supposed and real, it may be well to lay stress even
more than upon Shakespeare's.   If to our English
race an inadequate sense for perfection of work is
a real danger, if the discipline of respect for a high
and flawless excellence is peculiarly needed by us,
Milton is of all our gifted men the best lesson, the
most salutary influence.   In the sure and flawless
perfection of his rhythm and diction he is as
admirable as Virgil or Dante, and in this respect

he is unique amongst us. No one else in English literature and art possesses the like distinction.

Thomson, Cowper, Wordsworth, all of them
good poets who have studied Milton, followed
Milton, adopted his form, fail in their diction and
rhythm if we try them by that high standard of
excellence maintained by Milton constantly. From
style really high and pure Milton never departs ;
their departures from it are frequent.

Shakespeare is divinely strong, rich, and attractive. But sureness of perfect style Shakespeare
himself does not possess. I have heard a politician
express wonder at the treasures of political wisdom
in a certain celebrated scene of *Troilus and Cres-
sida ;* for my part I am at least equally moved to
wonder at the fantastic and false diction in which
Shakespeare has in that scene clothed them. Milton, from one end of *Paradise Lost* to the other, is in
his diction and rhythm constantly a great artist in
the great style. Whatever may be said as to the
subject of his poem, as to the conditions under

which he received his subject and treated it, that praise, at any rate, is assured to him.

For the rest, justice is not at present done, in my opinion, to Milton's management of the inevitable matter of a Puritan epic, a matter full of difficulties, for a poet. Justice is not done to the *architectonics*, as Goethe would have called them, of *Paradise Lost;* in these, too, the power of Milton's art is remarkable. But this may be a proposition which requires discussion and development for establishing it, and they are impossible on an occasion like the present.

That Milton, of all our English race, is by his diction and rhythm the one artist of the highest rank in the great style whom we have; this I take as requiring no discussion, this I take as certain.

The mighty power of poetry and art is generally admitted. But where the soul of this power, of this power at its best, chiefly resides, very many of us fail to see. It resides chiefly in the refining and elevation wrought in us by the high and rare excellence of the great style. We may feel the effect without being able to give ourselves clear account of its cause, but the thing is so. Now, no race needs the influences mentioned, the influences of refining and elevation, more than ours ; and in poetry and art our grand source for them is Milton.

To what does he owe this supreme distinction ? To nature first and foremost, to that bent of nature for inequality which to the worshippers of the average man is so unacceptable ; to a gift, a divine favour. 'The older one grows,' says Goethe, ' the more one prizes natural gifts, because by no possibility can they be procured and stuck on.' Nature formed Milton to be a great poet. But what other poet has shown so sincere a sense of the grandeur of his vocation, and a moral effort so constant and sublime to make and keep himself worthy of it ? The Milton of religious and political controversy, and perhaps of domestic life also, is not seldom disfigured by want of amenity, by acerbity. The Milton of poetry, on the other

hand, is one of those great men 'who are modest'
—to quote a fine remark of Leopardi, that gifted
and stricken young Italian, who in his sense for
poetic style is worthy to be named with Dante
and Milton—'who are modest, because they continually compare themselves, not with other men,
but with that idea of the perfect which they have
before their mind.' The Milton of poetry is the
man, in his own magnificent phrase, of 'devout
prayer to that Eternal Spirit that can enrich with
all utterance and knowledge, and sends out his
Seraphim with the hallowed fire of his altar, to
touch and purify the lips of whom he pleases.'
And finally, the Milton of poetry is, in his own
words again, the man of 'industrious and select
reading.' Continually he lived in companionship
with high and rare excellence, with the great
Hebrew poets and prophets, with the great poets
of Greece and Rome. The Hebrew compositions
were not in verse, and can be not inadequately
represented by the grand, measured prose of our
English Bible. The verse of the poets of Greece

F

and Rome no translation can adequately re-
produce. Prose cannot have the power of verse ;
verse-translation may give whatever of charm is
in the soul and talent of the translator himself,
but never the specific charm of the verse and poet
translated. In our race are thousands of readers,
presently there will be millions, who know not a
word of Greek and Latin, and will never learn
those languages. If this host of readers are ever
to gain any sense of the power and charm of the
great poets of antiquity, their way to gain it is not
through translations of the ancients, but through
the original poetry of Milton, who has the like
power and charm, because he has the like great
style.

Through Milton they may gain it, for, in conclusion, Milton is English; this master in the
great style of the ancients is English. Virgil,
whom Milton loved and honoured, has at the end
of the *Æneid* a noble passage, where Juno,
seeing the defeat of Turnus and the Italians
imminent, the victory of the Trojan invaders

assured, entreats Jupiter that Italy may nevertheless survive and be herself still, may retain her
own mind, manners, and language, and not adopt
those of the conqueror.

'Sit Latium, sint Albani per secula reges !

Jupiter grants the prayer; he promises perpetuity
and the future to Italy—Italy reinforced by whatever virtue the Trojan race has, but Italy, not
Troy. This we may take as a sort of parable
suiting ourselves. All the Anglo-Saxon contagion,
all the flood of Anglo-Saxon commonness, beats
vainly against the great style but cannot shake it,
and has to accept its triumph. But it triumphs
in Milton, in one of our own race, tongue, faith,
and morals. Milton has made the great style
no longer an exotic here; he has made it an
inmate amongst us, a leaven, and a power.
Nevertheless he, and his hearers on both sides
of the Atlantic, are English, and will remain
English—

'Sermonem Ausonii patrium moresque tenebunt.'

The English race overspreads the world, and at the same time the ideal of an excellence the most high and the most rare abides a possession with it for ever.

THOMAS GRAY[1]

JAMES BROWN, Master of Pembroke Hall at Cambridge, Gray's friend and executor, in a letter written a fortnight after Gray's death to another of his friends, Dr. Wharton of Old Park, Durham, has the following passage :—

'Everything is now dark and melancholy in Mr. Gray's room, not a trace of him remains there; it looks as if it had been for some time uninhabited, and the room bespoke for another inhabitant. The thoughts I have of him will last, and will be useful to me the few years I can expect to live. He never spoke out, but I believe from some little expressions I now re-

[1] Prefixed to the Selection from Gray in Ward's *English Poets*, vol. iv. 1880.

member to have dropped from him, that for some
time past he thought himself nearer his end than
those about him apprehended.'

He never spoke out. In these four words is
contained the whole history of Gray, both as a
man and as a poet. The words fell naturally, and
as it were by chance, from their writer's pen; but
let us dwell upon them, and press into their
meaning, for in following it we shall come to
understand Gray.

He was in his fifty-fifth year when he died,
and he lived in ease and leisure, yet a few pages
hold all his poetry; *he never spoke out* in poetry.
Still, the reputation which he has achieved by his
few pages is extremely high. True, Johnson
speaks of him with coldness and disparagement.
Gray disliked Johnson, and refused to make his
acquaintance; one might fancy that Johnson
wrote with some irritation from this cause. But
Johnson was not by nature fitted to do justice
to Gray and to his poetry; this by itself is a
sufficient explanation of the deficiencies of his

criticism of Gray. We may add a further explanation of them which is supplied by Mr. Cole's papers. 'When Johnson was publishing his Life of Gray,' says Mr. Cole, 'I gave him several anecdotes, *but he was very anxious as soon as possible to get to the end of his labours.*' Johnson was not naturally in sympathy with Gray, whose life he had to write, and when he wrote it he was in a hurry besides. He did Gray injustice, but even Johnson's authority failed to make injustice, in this case, prevail. Lord Macaulay calls the Life of Gray the worst of Johnson's Lives, and it had found many censurers before Macaulay. Gray's poetical reputation grew and flourished in spite of it. The poet Mason, his first biographer, in his epitaph equalled him with Pindar. Britain has known, says Mason,

'. . . a Homer's fire in Milton's strains,
A Pindar's rapture in the lyre of Gray.'

The immense vogue of Pope and of his style of versification had at first prevented the frank re-

ception of Gray by the readers of poetry. The
Elegy pleased; it could not but please: but
Gray's poetry, on the whole, astonished his contemporaries at first more than it pleased them; it
was so unfamiliar, so unlike the sort of poetry in
vogue. It made its way, however, after his death,
with the public as well as with the few; and
Gray's second biographer, Mitford, remarks that
'the works which were either neglected or
ridiculed by their contemporaries have now raised
Gray and Collins to the rank of our two greatest
lyric poets.' Their reputation was established, at
any rate, and stood extremely high, even if they
were not popularly read. Johnson's disparagement of Gray was called 'petulant,' and severely
blamed. Beattie, at the end of the eighteenth
century, writing to Sir William Forbes, says: 'Of
all the English poets of this age Mr. Gray is most
admired, and I think with justice.' Cowper
writes: 'I have been reading Gray's works, and
think him the only poet since Shakespeare en-
titled to the character of sublime. Perhaps you

will remember that I once had a different opinion
of him. I was prejudiced.' Adam Smith says :
'Gray joins to the sublimity of Milton the
elegance and harmony of Pope; and nothing is
wanting to render him, perhaps, the first poet in
the English language, but to have written a little
more.' And, to come nearer to our own times,
Sir James Mackintosh speaks of Gray thus : 'Of
all English poets he was the most finished artist.
He attained the highest degree of splendour of
which poetical style seemed to be capable.'

In a poet of such magnitude, how shall we
explain his scantiness of production ? Shall we
explain it by saying that to make of Gray a poet
of this magnitude is absurd ; that his genius and
resources were small, and that his production,
therefore, was small also, but that the popularity
of a single piece, the *Elegy*,—a popularity due in
great measure to the subject,—created for Gray
a reputation to which he has really no right ?
He himself was not deceived by the favour shown
to the *Elegy*. 'Gray told me with a good deal of

acrimony,' writes Dr. Gregory, 'that the *Elegy*
owed its popularity entirely to the subject, and
that the public would have received it as well if
it had been written in prose.' This is too much
to say ; the *Elegy* is a beautiful poem, and in
admiring it the public showed a true feeling for
poetry. But it is true that the *Elegy* owed
much of its success to its subject, and that it has
received a too unmeasured and unbounded praise.

Gray himself, however, maintained that the
Elegy was not his best work in poetry, and he was
right. High as is the praise due to the *Elegy*, it
is yet true that in other productions of Gray he
exhibits poetical qualities even higher than those
exhibited in the *Elegy*. He deserves, therefore,
his extremely high reputation as a poet, although
his critics and the public may not always have
praised him with perfect judgment. We are
brought back, then, to the question : How, in a
poet so really considerable, are we to explain his
scantiness of production ?

Scanty Gray's production, indeed, is ; so scanty

that to supplement our knowledge of it by a knowledge of the man is in this case of peculiar interest and service. Gray's letters and the records of him by his friends have happily made it possible for us thus to know him, and to appreciate his high qualities of mind and soul. Let us see these in the man first, and then observe how they appear in his poetry; and why they cannot enter into it more freely and inspire it with more strength, render it more abundant.

We will begin with his acquirements. 'Mr. Gray was,' writes his friend Temple, 'perhaps the most learned man in Europe. He knew every branch of history both natural and civil; had read all the original historians of England, France, and Italy; and was a great antiquarian. Criticism, metaphysics, morals, politics, made a principal part of his study. Voyages and travels of all sorts were his favourite amusements; and he had a fine taste in painting, prints, architecture, and gardening.' The notes in his interleaved copy of Linnæus remained to show the extent and accuracy of his knowledge in the natural sciences, particularly in botany, zoology, and entomology. Entomologists testified that his account of English insects was more perfect than any that had then appeared. His notes and papers, of which some have been published, others remain still in manuscript, give evidence, besides, of his knowledge of literature ancient and modern, geography and topography, painting, architecture and antiquities, and of his curious researches in heraldry. He was an excellent musician. Sir James Mackintosh reminds us, moreover, that to all the other accomplishments and merits of Gray we are to add this : ' That he was the first discoverer of the beauties of nature in England, and has marked out the course of every picturesque journey that can be made in it.'

Acquirements take all their value and character from the power of the individual storing them. Let us take, from amongst Gray's observations on what he read, enough to show us his power. Here are criticisms on three very different

authors, criticisms without any study or pretension, but just thrown out in chance letters to his
friends. First, on Aristotle :—

' In the first place he is the hardest author by far
I ever meddled with. Then he has a dry conciseness
that makes one imagine one is perusing a table of
contents rather than a book ; it tastes for all the
world like chopped hay, or rather like chopped logic ;
for he has a violent affection to that art, being in
some sort his own invention ; so that he often loses
himself in little trifling distinctions and verbal
niceties, and what is worse, leaves you to extricate
yourself as you can. Thirdly, he has suffered vastly
by his transcribers, as all authors of great brevity
necessarily must. Fourthly and lastly, he has abundance of fine, uncommon things, which make him
well worth the pains he gives one. You see what
you have to expect.'

Next, on Isocrates :—

' It would be strange if I should find fault with
you for reading Isocrates ; I did so myself twenty
years ago, and in an edition at least as bad as
yours. The Panegyric, the De Pace, Areopagitic,
and Advice to Philip, are by far the noblest remains
we have of this writer, and equal to most things
extant in the Greek tongue ; but it depends on your
judgment to distinguish between his real and occa-

sional opinion of things, as he directly contradicts
in one place what he has advanced in another ; for
example, in the Panathenaic and the De Pace, on the
naval power of Athens ; the latter of the two is
undoubtedly his own undisguised sentiment.'

After hearing Gray on Isocrates and Aristotle,
let us hear him on Froissart :—

'I rejoice you have met with Froissart, he is the
Herodotus of a barbarous age ; had he but had the
luck of writing in as good a language, he might have
been immortal. His locomotive disposition (for
then there was no other way of learning things), his
simple curiosity, his religious credulity, were much
like those of the old Grecian. When you have *tant
chevauché* as to get to the end of him, there is
Monstrelet waits to take you up, and will set you
down at Philip de Commines ; but previous to all
these, you should have read Villehardouin and
Joinville.'

Those judgments, with their true and clear
ring, evince the high quality of Gray's mind, his
power to command and use his learning. But
Gray was a poet ; let us hear him on a poet, on
Shakespeare. We must place ourselves in the
full midst of the eighteenth century and of its

criticism ; Gray's friend, West, had praised Racine
for using in his dramas 'the language of the
times and that of the purest sort' ; and he had
added : 'I will not decide what style is fit for our
English stage, but I should rather choose one that
bordered upon Cato, than upon Shakespeare.'
Gray replies :—

'As to matter of style, I have this to say : The
language of the age is never the language of poetry ;
except among the French, whose verse, where the
thought does not support it, differs in nothing from
prose. Our poetry, on the contrary, has a language
peculiar to itself, to which almost every one that
has written has added something. In truth, Shakespeare's language is one of his principal beauties ;
and he has no less advantage over your Addisons
and Rowes in this, than in those other great
excellences you mention. Every word in him is a
picture. Pray put me the following lines into the
tongue of our modern dramatics—

'"But I, that am not shaped for sportive tricks,
    Nor made to court an amorous looking-glass"—

and what follows ? To me they appear untranslatable ; and if this be the case, our language is greatly
degenerated.'

It is impossible for a poet to lay down the rules of his own art with more insight, soundness, and certainty. Yet at that moment in England there was perhaps not one other man, besides Gray, capable of writing the passage just quoted.

Gray's quality of mind, then, we see; his quality of soul will no less bear inspection. His reserve, his delicacy, his distaste for many of the persons and things surrounding him in the Cambridge of that day,—'this silly, dirty place,' as he calls it,—have produced an impression of Gray as being a man falsely fastidious, finical, effeminate. But we have already had that grave testimony to him from the Master of Pembroke Hall : 'The thoughts I have of him will last, and will be useful to me the few years I can expect to live.' And here is another to the same effect from a younger man, from Gray's friend Nicholls :—

'You know,' he writes to his mother, from abroad, when he heard of Gray's death, 'that I considered Mr. Gray as a second parent, that I thought only of him, built all my happiness on him, talked of him for ever, wished him with me whenever I partook of any pleasure, and flew to him for refuge whenever I felt any uneasiness. To whom now shall I talk of all I have seen here? Who will teach me to read, to think, to feel? I protest to you, that whatever I did or thought had a reference to him. If I met with any chagrins, I comforted myself that I had a treasure at home; if all the world had despised and hated me, I should have thought myself perfectly recompensed in his friendship. There remains only one loss more; if I lose you, I am left alone in the world. At present I feel that I have lost half of myself.'

Testimonies such as these are not called forth by a fastidious effeminate weakling; they are not called forth, even, by mere qualities of mind; they are called forth by qualities of soul. And of Gray's high qualities of soul, of his σπουδαιότης, his excellent seriousness, we may gather abundant proof from his letters. Writing to Mason who had just lost his father, he says:—

'I have seen the scene you describe, and know how dreadful it is; I know too I am the better for it. We are all idle and thoughtless things, and have no sense, no use in the world any longer than that sad impression lasts; the deeper it is engraved the better.'

G

And again, on a like occasion to another friend :—

'He who best knows our nature (for he made us what we are) by such afflictions recalls us from our wandering thoughts and idle merriment, from the insolence of youth and prosperity, to serious reflection, to our duty, and to himself; nor need we hasten to get rid of these impressions. Time (by appointment of the same Power) will cure the smart and in some hearts soon blot out all the traces of sorrow ; but such as preserve them longest (for it is partly left in our own power) do perhaps best acquiesce in the will of the chastiser.'

And once more to Mason, in the very hour of his wife's death; Gray was not sure whether or not his letter would reach Mason before the end :—

'If the worst be not yet past, you will neglect and pardon me ; but if the last struggle be over, if the poor object of your long anxieties be no longer sensible to your kindness or to her own sufferings, allow me, at least an idea (for what could I do, were I present, more than this?) to sit by you in silence and pity from my heart not her, who is at rest, but you, who lose her. May he, who made us, the Master of our pleasures and of our pains, support you ! Adieu.'

Seriousness, character, was the foundation of things with him ; where this was lacking he was always severe, whatever might be offered to him in its stead. Voltaire's literary genius charmed him, but the faults of Voltaire's nature he felt so strongly that when his young friend Nicholls was going abroad in 1771, just before Gray's death, he said to him : 'I have one thing to beg of you which you must not refuse.' Nicholls answered : 'You know you have only to command ; what is it ?'——' Do not go to see Voltaire,' said Gray ; and then added : 'No one knows the mischief that man will do.' Nicholls promised compliance with Gray's injunction ; 'But what,' he asked, 'could a visit from me signify ?'——'Every tribute to such a man signifies,' Gray answered. He admired Dryden, admired him, even, too much ; had too much felt his influence as a poet. He told Beattie 'that if there was any excellence in his own numbers he had learned it wholly from that great poet' ; and writing to Beattie afterwards he recurs to Dryden, whom Beattie, he thought, did not honour enough as a poet : 'Remember Dryden,' he writes, 'and be blind to all his faults.' Yes, his faults as a poet; but on the man Dryden, nevertheless, his sentence is stern. Speaking of the Poet-Laureateship, 'Dryden,' he writes to Mason, 'was as disgraceful to the office from his character, as the poorest scribbler could have been from his verses.' Even where crying blemishes were absent, the want of weight and depth of character in a man deprived him, in Gray's judgment, of serious significance. He says of Hume : 'Is not that *naïveté* and good-humour, which his admirers celebrate in him, owing to this, that he has continued all his days an infant, but one that has unhappily been taught to read and write ?'

And with all this strenuous seriousness, a pathetic sentiment, and an element, likewise, of sportive and charming humour. At Keswick, by the lakeside on an autumn evening, he has the accent of the *Rêveries*, or of Obermann, or Wordsworth :—

'In the evening walked down alone to the lake by the side of Crow Park after sunset and saw the

solemn colouring of light draw on, the last gleam of
sunshine fading away on the hill-tops, the deep serene
of the waters, and the long shadows of the mountains
thrown across them, till they nearly touched the
hithermost shore.   At distance heard the murmur
of many waterfalls, not audible in the daytime.
Wished for the Moon, but she was *dark to me and
silent, hid in her vacant interlunar cave.*'

Of his humour and sportiveness his delightful
letters are full ; his humour appears in his poetry
too, and is by no means to be passed over there.
Horace Walpole said that ' Gray never wrote
anything easily but things of humour ; humour
was his natural and original turn.'

Knowledge, penetration, seriousness, sentiment,
humour, Gray had them all ; he had the equipment
and endowment for the office of poet.   But very
soon in his life appear traces of something obstructing, something disabling ; of spirits failing,
and health not sound ; and the evil increases with
years.   He writes to West in 1737 :—

' Low spirits are my true and faithful companions ;
they get up with me, go to bed with me, make
journeys and returns as I do ; nay, and pay visits

and will even affect to be jocose and force a feeble laugh with me; but most commonly we sit alone together, and are the prettiest insipid company in the world.'

The tone is playful, Gray was not yet twenty-one. 'Mine,' he tells West four or five years later, 'mine, you are to know, is a white Melancholy, or rather *Leucocholy*, for the most part; which, though it seldom laughs or dances, nor ever amounts to what one calls joy or pleasure, yet is a good easy sort of a state.' But, he adds in this same letter :—

'But there is another sort, black indeed, which I have now and then felt, that has something in it like Tertullian's rule of faith, *Credo quia impossibile est;* for it believes, nay, is sure of everything that is unlikely, so it be but frightful; and on the other hand excludes and shuts its eyes to the most possible hopes, and everything that is pleasurable; from this the Lord deliver us! for none but he and sunshiny weather can do it.'

Six or seven years pass, and we find him writing to Wharton from Cambridge thus :—

'The spirit of laziness (the spirit of this place) begins to possess even me, that have so long declaimed

against it. Yet has it not so prevailed, but that I
feel that discontent with myself, that *ennui*, that ever
accompanies it in its beginnings. Time will settle
my conscience, time will reconcile my languid companion to me ; we shall smoke, we shall tipple, we
shall doze together, we shall have our little jokes, like
other people, and our long stories. Brandy will
finish what port began ; and, a month after the time,
you will see in some corner of a London Evening
Post, "Yesterday died the Rev. Mr. John Gray,
Senior-Fellow of Clare Hall, a facetious companion,
and well-respected by all who knew him." '

The humorous advertisement ends, in the original letter, with a Hogarthian touch which I
must not quote. Is it Leucocholy or is it Melancholy which predominates here ? at any rate,
this entry in his diary, six years later, is black
enough :—

  ' *Insomnia crebra, atque expergiscenti surdus quidam
doloris sensus ; frequens etiam in regione sterni oppressio,
et cardialgia gravis, fere sempiterna.*'

And in 1757 he writes to Hurd :—

  'To be employed is to be happy. This principle
of mine (and I am convinced of its truth) has, as
usual, no influence on my practice. I am alone, and

ennuyé to the last degree, yet do nothing. Indeed I
have one excuse; my health (which you have so
kindly inquired after) is not extraordinary. It is no
great malady, but several little ones, that seem brew-
ing no good to me.'

From thence to the end his languor and depression, though still often relieved by occupation
and travel, keep fatally gaining on him. At last
the depression became constant, became mechanical. 'Travel I must,' he writes to Dr. Wharton,
'or cease to exist. Till this year I hardly knew
what *mechanical* low spirits were; but now I even
tremble at an east wind.' Two months afterwards
he died.

What wonder, that with this troublous cloud,
throughout the whole term of his manhood, brood-
ing over him and weighing him down, Gray, finely
endowed though he was, richly stored with knowledge though he was, yet produced so little, found
no full and sufficient utterance, '*never*,' as the
Master of Pembroke Hall said, '*spoke out.*' He
knew well enough, himself, how it was with him.

'My *verve* is at best, you know' (he writes to

Mason), 'of so delicate a constitution, and has such weak nerves, as not to stir out of its chamber above three days in a year.' And to Horace Walpole he says: 'As to what you say to me civilly, that I ought to write more, I will be candid, and avow to you, that till fourscore and upward, whenever the humour takes me, I will write; because I like it, and because I like myself better when I do so. If I do not write much, it is because I cannot.' How simply said, and how truly also! Fain would a man like Gray speak out if he could, he 'likes himself better' when he speaks out; if he does not speak out, 'it is because I cannot.'

Bonstetten, that mercurial Swiss who died in 1832 at the age of eighty - seven, having been younger and livelier from his sixtieth year to his eightieth than at any other time in his life, paid a visit in his early days to Cambridge, and saw much of Gray, to whom he attached himself with devotion. Gray, on his part, was charmed with his young friend; 'I never saw such a boy,' he writes; 'our breed is not made on this model.' Long afterwards Bonstetten published his reminiscences of Gray. ' I used to tell Gray,' he says, ' about my life and my native country, but *his* life was a sealed book to me ; he never would talk of himself, never would allow me to speak to him of his poetry. If I quoted lines of his to him, he kept silence like an obstinate child. I said to him sometimes : " Will you have the goodness to give me an answer ? " But not a word issued from his lips.' *He never spoke out.* Bonstetten thinks that Gray's life was poisoned by an unsatisfied sensibility, was withered by his having never loved ; by his days being passed in the dismal cloisters of Cambridge, in the company of a set of monastic book-worms, ' whose existence no honest woman ever came to cheer.' Sainte-Beuve, who was much attracted and interested by Gray, doubts whether Bonstetten's explanation of him is admissible ; the secret of Gray's melancholy he finds rather in the sterility of his poetic talent, ' so distinguished, so rare, but so stinted ' ; in the poet's despair at his own unproductiveness.

But to explain Gray, we must do more than allege his sterility, as we must look further than to his reclusion at Cambridge. What caused his sterility? Was it his ill-health, his hereditary gout? Certainly we will pay all respect to the powers of hereditary gout for afflicting us poor mortals. But Goethe, after pointing out that Schiller, who was so productive, was 'almost constantly ill,' adds the true remark that it is incredible how much the spirit can do, in these cases, to keep up the body. Pope's animation and activity through all the course of what he pathetically calls 'that long disease, my life,' is an example presenting itself signally, in Gray's own country and time, to confirm what Goethe here says. What gave the power to Gray's reclusion and ill-health to induce his sterility?

The reason, the indubitable reason as I cannot but think it, I have already given elsewhere. Gray, a born poet, fell upon an age of prose. He fell upon an age whose task was such as to call forth in general men's powers of understanding,

wit and cleverness, rather than their deepest
powers of mind and soul. As regards literary
production, the task of the eighteenth century in
England was not the poetic interpretation of the
world, its task was to create a plain, clear, straight-
forward, efficient prose. Poetry obeyed the bent
of mind requisite for the due fulfilment of this
task of the century. It was intellectual, argumentative, ingenious; not seeing things in their
truth and beauty, not interpretative. Gray, with
the qualities of mind and soul of a genuine poet,
was isolated in his century. Maintaining and
fortifying them by lofty studies, he yet could not
fully educe and enjoy them ; the want of a genial
atmosphere, the failure of sympathy in his contemporaries, were too great. Born in the same
year with Milton, Gray would have been another
man ; born in the same year with Burns, he would
have been another man. A man born in 1608
could profit by the larger and more poetic scope
of the English spirit in the Elizabethan age ; a
man born in 1759 could profit by that European

renewing of men's minds of which the great historical manifestation is the French Revolution. Gray's alert and brilliant young friend, Bonstetten, who would explain the void in the life of Gray by his having never loved, Bonstetten himself loved, married, and had children. Yet at the age of fifty he was bidding fair to grow old, dismal and torpid like the rest of us, when he was roused and made young again for some thirty years, says M. Sainte-Beuve, by the events of 1789. If Gray, like Burns, had been just thirty years old when the French Revolution broke out, he would have shown, probably, productiveness and animation in plenty. Coming when he did, and endowed as he was, he was a man born out of date, a man whose full spiritual flowering was impossible. The same thing is to be said of his great contemporary, Butler, the author of the *Analogy*. In the sphere of religion, which touches that of poetry, Butler was impelled by the endowment of his nature to strive for a profound and adequate conception of religious things, which was not pursued by his

contemporaries, and which at that time, and in
that atmosphere of mind, was not fully attainable.
Hence, in Butler too, a dissatisfaction, a weariness,
as in Gray ; 'great labour and weariness, great
disappointment, pain and even vexation of mind.'
A sort of spiritual east wind was at that time
blowing; neither Butler nor Gray could flower.
They *never spoke out.*

Gray's poetry was not only stinted in quantity
by reason of the age wherein he lived, it suffered
somewhat in quality also.   We have seen under
what obligation to Dryden Gray professed himself to be—' if there was any excellence in his
numbers, he had learned it wholly from that great
poet.'   It was not for nothing that he came when
Dryden had lately 'embellished,' as Johnson says,
English poetry ; had 'found it brick and left it
marble.'   It was not for nothing that he came just
when 'the English ear,' to quote Johnson again,
' had been accustomed to the mellifluence of Pope's
numbers, and the diction of poetry had grown
more splendid.'   Of the intellectualities, inge-

nuities, personifications, of the movement and diction of Dryden and Pope, Gray caught something,
caught too much. We have little of Gray's poetry,
and that little is not free from the faults of his
age. Therefore it was important to go for aid, as
we did, to Gray's life and letters, to see his mind
and soul there, and to corroborate from thence that
high estimate of his quality which his poetry indeed calls forth, but does not establish so amply
and irresistibly as one could desire.

For a just criticism it does, however, clearly
establish it. The difference between genuine
poetry and the poetry of Dryden, Pope, and all
their school, is briefly this : their poetry is conceived and composed in their wits, genuine poetry
is conceived and composed in the soul. The difference between the two kinds of poetry is immense.
They differ profoundly in their modes of language,
they differ profoundly in their modes of evolution.
The poetic language of our eighteenth century in
general is the language of men composing *without
their eye on the object*, as Wordsworth excellently

said of Dryden; language merely recalling the object, as the common language of prose does, and then dressing it out with a certain smartness and brilliancy for the fancy and understanding. This is called 'splendid diction.' The evolution of the poetry of our eighteenth century is likewise intellectual; it proceeds by ratiocination, antithesis, ingenious turns and conceits. This poetry is often eloquent, and always, in the hands of such masters as Dryden and Pope, clever; but it does not take us much below the surface of things, it does not give us the emotion of seeing things in their truth and beauty. The language of genuine poetry, on the other hand, is the language of one composing with his eye on the object; its evolution is that of a thing which has been plunged in the poet's soul until it comes forth naturally and necessarily. This sort of evolution is infinitely simpler than the other, and infinitely more satisfying; the same thing is true of the genuine poetic language likewise. But they are both of them also infinitely harder of attainment; they come only from those who, as Emerson says, 'live from a great depth of being.'

Goldsmith disparaged Gray who had praised his *Traveller*, and indeed in the poem on the *Alliance of Education and Government* had given him hints which he used for it. In retaliation let us take from Goldsmith himself a specimen of the poetic language of the eighteenth century.

'No cheerful murmurs fluctuate in the gale'—

there is exactly the poetic diction of our prose century ! rhetorical, ornate,—and, poetically, quite false. Place beside it a line of genuine poetry, such as the

'In cradle of the rude, imperious surge'

of Shakespeare ; and all its falseness instantly becomes apparent.

Dryden's poem on the death of Mrs. Killigrew is, says Johnson, 'undoubtedly the noblest ode that our language ever has produced.' In this vigorous performance Dryden has to say, what is interesting enough, that not only in poetry did

Mrs. Killigrew excel, but she excelled in painting also. And thus he says it—

> 'To the next realm she stretch'd her sway,
> For Painture near adjoining lay—
> A plenteous province and alluring prey.
> A Chamber of Dependencies was framed
> (As conquerors will never want pretence
> When arm'd, to justify the offence),
> And the whole fief, in right of Poetry, she claim'd.'

The intellectual, ingenious, superficial evolution of poetry of this school could not be better illustrated. Place beside it Pindar's

> αἰὼν ἀσφαλὴς
> οὐκ ἔγεντ' οὔτ' Αἰακίδᾳ παρὰ Πηλεῖ,
> οὔτε παρ' ἀντιθέῳ Κάδμῳ . . .

'A secure time fell to the lot neither of Peleus the son of Æacus, nor of the godlike Cadmus; howbeit these are said to have had, of all mortals, the supreme of happiness, who heard the golden-snooded Muses sing,—on the mountain the one heard them, the other in seven-gated Thebes.'

There is the evolution of genuine poetry, and such poetry kills Dryden's the moment it is put near it.

Gray's production was scanty, and scanty, as we have seen, it could not but be. Even what he produced is not always pure in diction, true in evolution. Still, with whatever drawbacks, he is alone, or almost alone (for Collins has something of the like merit) in his age. Gray said himself that 'the style he aimed at was extreme conciseness of expression, yet pure, perspicuous, and musical.' Compared, not with the work of the great masters of the golden ages of poetry, but with the poetry of his own contemporaries in general, Gray's may be said to have reached, in style, the excellence at which he aimed ; while the evolution also of such a piece as his *Progress of Poesy* must be accounted not less noble and sound than its style.

IV

JOHN KEATS[1]

POETRY, according to Milton's famous saying, should be 'simple, sensuous, impassioned.' No one can question the eminency, in Keats's poetry, of the quality of sensuousness. Keats as a poet is abundantly and enchantingly sensuous; the question with some people will be, whether he is anything else. •Many things may be brought forward which seem to show him as under the fascination and sole dominion of sense, and desiring nothing better. There is the exclamation in one of his letters : 'O for a life of sensations rather than of thoughts!' There is the thesis, in another, 'that with a great Poet the sense of Beauty overcomes

[1] Prefixed to the Selection from Keats in Ward's *English Poets*, vol. iv. 1880.

every other consideration, or rather obliterates all
consideration.' There is Haydon's story of him,
how ' he once covered his tongue and throat as far
as he could reach with Cayenne pepper, in order
to appreciate the delicious coldness of claret in
all its glory—his own expression.' One is not
much surprised when Haydon further tells us, of
the hero of such a story, that once for six weeks
together he was hardly ever sober. 'He had no
decision of character,' Haydon adds; 'no object
upon which to direct his great powers.'

Character and self-control, the *virtus verusque
labor* so necessary for every kind of greatness, and
for the great artist, too, indispensable, appear to
be wanting, certainly, to this Keats of Haydon's
portraiture. They are wanting also to the Keats
of the *Letters to Fanny Brawne*. These letters
make as unpleasing an impression as Haydon's
anecdotes. The editor of Haydon's journals could
not well omit what Haydon said of his friend, but
for the publication of the *Letters to Fanny Brawne*
I can see no good reason whatever. Their publi-

cation appears to me, I confess, inexcusable; they ought never to have been published. But published they are, and we have to take notice of them. Letters written when Keats was near his end, under the throttling and unmanning grasp of mortal disease, we will not judge. But here is a letter written some months before he was taken ill. It is printed just as Keats wrote it.

'You have absorb'd me. I have a sensation at the present moment as though I was dissolving—I should be exquisitely miserable without the hope of soon seeing you. I should be afraid to separate myself far from you. My sweet Fanny, will your heart never change? My love, will it? I have no limit now to my love. . . . Your note came in just here. I cannot be happier away from you. 'Tis richer than an Argosy of Pearles. Do not threat me even in jest. I have been astonished that Men could die Martyrs for religion—I have shuddered at it. I shudder no more—I could be martyred for my Religion—Love is my religion—I could die for that. I could die for you. My Creed is Love and you are its only tenet. You have ravished me away by a Power I cannot resist; and yet I could resist till I saw you; and even since I have seen you I have endeavoured often "to reason against the reasons of my Love." I can do that no more—the pain would be too great. My love is selfish. I cannot breathe without you.'

A man who writes love-letters in this strain is probably predestined, one may observe, to misfortune in his love-affairs; but that is nothing. The complete enervation of the writer is the real point for remark. We have the tone, or rather the entire want of tone, the abandonment of all reticence and all dignity, of the merely sensuous man, of the man who 'is passion's slave.' Nay, we have them in such wise that one is tempted to speak even as *Blackwood* or the *Quarterly* were in the old days wont to speak ; one is tempted to say that Keats's love-letter is the love-letter of a surgeon's apprentice. It has in its relaxed self-abandonment something underbred and ignoble, as of a youth ill brought up, without the training which teaches us that we must put some constraint upon our feelings and upon the expression of them. It is the sort of love-letter of a surgeon's apprentice which one might hear read out in a breach of promise case, or in the Divorce Court.

The sensuous man speaks in it, and the sensuous man of a badly bred and badly trained sort. That many who are themselves also badly bred and badly trained should enjoy it, and should even think it a beautiful and characteristic production of him whom they call their 'lovely and beloved Keats,' does not make it better. These are the admirers whose pawing and fondness does not good but harm to the fame of Keats; who concentrate attention upon what in him is least wholesome and most questionable ; who worship him, and would have the world worship him too, as the poet of

'Light feet, dark violet eyes, and parted hair,
  Soft dimpled hands, white neck, and creamy breast.

This sensuous strain Keats had, and a man of his poetic powers could not, whatever his strain, but show his talent in it. But he has something more, and something better. We who believe Keats to have been by his promise, at any rate, if not fully by his performance, one of the very greatest of

English poets, and who believe also that a merely sensuous man cannot either by promise or by performance be a very great poet, because poetry interprets life, and so large and noble a part of life is outside of such a man's ken,—we cannot but look for signs in him of something more than sensuousness, for signs of character and virtue. And indeed the elements of high character Keats undoubtedly has, and the effort to develop them ; the effort is frustrated and cut short by misfortune, and disease, and time, but for the due understanding of Keats's worth the recognition of this effort, and of the elements on which it worked, is necessary.

Lord Houghton, who praises very discriminatingly the poetry of Keats, has on his character also a remark full of discrimination. He says : 'The faults of Keats's disposition were precisely the contrary of those attributed to him by common opinion.' And he gives a letter written after the death of Keats by his brother George, in which the writer, speaking of the fantastic *Johnny Keats*

invented for common opinion by Lord Byron and
by the reviewers, declares indignantly : ' John was
the very soul of manliness and courage, and as
much like the Holy Ghost as *Johnny Keats.*' It
is important to note this testimony, and to look
well for whatever illustrates and confirms it.

Great weight is laid by Lord Houghton on
such a direct profession of faith as the following :
' That sort of probity and disinterestedness,' Keats
writes to his brothers, ' which such men as Bailey
possess, does hold and grasp the tip-top of any
spiritual honours that can be paid to anything in
this world.' Lord Houghton says that ' never
have words more effectively expressed the conviction of the superiority of virtue above beauty
than those.' But merely to make a profession of
faith of the kind here made by Keats is not difficult ; what we should rather look for is some
evidence of the instinct for character, for virtue,
passing into the man's life, passing into his work.

Signs of virtue, in the true and large sense of
the word, the instinct for virtue passing into the

life of Keats and strengthening it, I find in the
admirable wisdom and temper of what he says
to his friend Bailey on the occasion of a quarrel
between Reynolds and Haydon :—

'Things have happened lately of great perplexity;
you must have heard of them; Reynolds and Haydon retorting and recriminating, and parting for
ever. The same thing has happened between Haydon and Hunt. It is unfortunate; men should bear
with each other; there lives not the man who may
not be cut up, aye, lashed to pieces, on his weakest
side. The best of men have but a portion of good
in them. . . . The sure way, Bailey, is first to know
a man's faults, and then be passive. If, after that,
he insensibly draws you towards him, then you have
no power to break the link. Before I felt interested
in either Reynolds or Haydon, I was well read in
their faults; yet, knowing them, I have been cement-
ing gradually with both. I have an affection for
them both, for reasons almost opposite; and to both
must I of necessity cling, supported always by the
hope that when a little time, a few years, shall have
tried me more fully in their esteem, I may be able to
bring them together.'

Butler has well said that 'endeavouring to
enforce upon our own minds a practical sense of
virtue, or to beget in others that practical sense of

it which a man really has himself, is a virtuous
act.' And such an 'endeavouring' is that of Keats
in those words written to Bailey. It is more
than mere words; so justly thought and so dis-
creetly urged as it is, it rises to the height of a
virtuous *act*. It is proof of character.

The same thing may be said of some words
written to his friend Charles Brown, whose kindness, willingly exerted whenever Keats chose to
avail himself of it, seemed to free him from any
pressing necessity of earning his own living.
Keats felt that he must not allow this state of
things to continue. He determined to set himself to 'fag on as others do' at periodical literature,
rather than to endanger his independence and his
self-respect ; and he writes to Brown :—

'I had got into a habit of mind of looking towards
you as a help in all difficulties. This very habit
would be the parent of idleness and difficulties. You
will see it is a duty I owe to myself to break the
neck of it. I do nothing for my subsistence—make
no exertion. At the end of another year you shall
applaud me, not for verses, but for conduct.'

He had not, alas, another year of health before
him when he announced that wholesome resolve ;
it then wanted but six months of the day of his
fatal attack. But in the brief time allowed to
him he did what he could to keep his word.

What character, again, what strength and clearness of judgment, in his criticism of his own productions, of the public, and of 'the literary circles'!
His words after the severe reviews of *Endymion*
have often been quoted ; they cannot be quoted
too often :—

'Praise or blame has but a momentary effect on
the man whose love of beauty in the abstract makes
him a severe critic on his own works. My own
criticism has given me pain without comparison beyond what *Blackwood* or the *Quarterly* could possibly
inflict ; and also, when I feel I am right, no external
praise can give me such a glow as my own solitary
reperception and ratification of what is fine. J. S. is
perfectly right in regard to the "slip-shod Endymion."
That it is so is no fault of mine. No ! though it
may sound a little paradoxical, it is as good as I had
power to make it by myself.'

And again, as if he had foreseen certain of his

admirers gushing over him, and was resolved to disengage his responsibility :—

'I have done nothing, except for the amusement of a few people who refine upon their feelings till anything in the un-understandable way will go down with them.   I have no cause to complain, because I am certain anything really fine will in these days be felt.   I have no doubt that if I had written *Othello* I should have been cheered.   I shall go on with patience.'

Young poets almost inevitably over-rate what they call 'the might of poesy,' and its power over the world which now is.   Keats is not a dupe on this matter any more than he is a dupe about the merit of his own performances :—

'I have no trust whatever in poetry.   I don't wonder at it ; the marvel is to me how people read so much of it.'

His attitude towards the public is that of a strong man, not of a weakling avid of praise, and made to 'be snuff'd out by an article' :—

'I shall ever consider the public as debtors to me for verses, not myself to them for admiration, which I can do without.'

And again, in a passage where one may perhaps find fault with the capital letters, but surely with nothing else :—

'I have not the slightest feel of humility towards the public or to anything in existence but the Eternal Being, the Principle of Beauty, and the Memory of great Men. . . . I would be subdued before my friends, and thank them for subduing me ; but among multitudes of men I have no feel of stooping ; I hate the idea of humility to them. I never wrote one single line of poetry with the least shadow of thought about their opinion. Forgive me for vexing you, but it eases me to tell you : I could not live without the love of my friends ; I would jump down Etna for any great public good—but I hate a mawkish popularity. I cannot be subdued before them. My glory would be to daunt and dazzle the thousand jabberers about pictures and books.'

Against these artistic and literary 'jabberers,' amongst whom Byron fancied Keats, probably, to be always living, flattering them and flattered by them, he has yet another outburst :—

'Just so much as I am humbled by the genius above my grasp, am I exalted and look with hate and contempt upon the literary world. Who could wish to be among the commonplace crowd of the little famous, who are each individually lost in a throng made up of themselves ?'

And he loves Fanny Brawne the more, he tells her, because he believes that she has liked him for his own sake and for nothing else. 'I have met with women who I really think would like to be married to a Poem and to be given away by a Novel.'

There is a tone of too much bitterness and defiance in all this, a tone which he with great propriety subdued and corrected when he wrote his beautiful preface to *Endymion*. But the thing to be seized is, that Keats had flint and iron in him, that he had character; that he was, as his brother George says, 'as much like the Holy Ghost as *Johnny Keats*,'—as that imagined sensuous weakling, the delight of the literary circles of Hampstead.

It is a pity that Byron, who so misconceived Keats, should never have known how shrewdly Keats, on the other hand, had characterised *him*.

as 'a fine thing' in the sphere of 'the worldly, theatrical, and pantomimical.' But indeed nothing is more remarkable in Keats than his clear-sightedness, his lucidity ; and lucidity is in itself akin to character and to high and severe work. In spite, therefore, of his overpowering feeling for beauty, in spite of his sensuousness, in spite of his facility, in spite of his gift of expression, Keats could say resolutely :—

'I know nothing, I have read nothing; and I mean to follow Solomon's directions : "Get learning, get understanding." There is but one way for me. The road lies through application, study, and thought. I will pursue it.'

And of Milton, instead of resting in Milton's incomparable phrases, Keats could say, although indeed all the while 'looking upon fine phrases,' as he himself tells us, 'like a lover'—

'Milton had an exquisite passion for what is properly, in the sense of ease and pleasure, poetical luxury ; and with that, it appears to me, he would fain nave been content, if he could, so doing, preserve his self-respect and feeling of duty performed ; but there was working in him, as it were, that same sort of thing which operates in the great world to the end of a prophecy's being accomplished. Therefore he devoted himself rather to the ardours than the pleasures of song, solacing himself at intervals with cups of old wine.'

In his own poetry, too, Keats felt that place must be found for 'the ardours rather than the pleasures of song,' although he was aware that he was not yet ripe for it—

'But my flag is not unfurl'd
On the Admiral-staff, and to philosophise
I dare not yet.'

Even in his pursuit of 'the pleasures of song,' however, there is that stamp of high work which is akin to character, which is character passing into intellectual production. *'The best sort of poetry*—that,' he truly says, ' is all I care for, all I live for.' It is curious to observe how this severe addiction of his to the best sort of poetry affects him with a certain coldness, as if the addiction had been to mathematics, towards those prime objects of a sensuous and passionate poet's regard, love and women. He speaks of 'the opinion I have formed of the generality of women, who appear to me as children to whom I would rather give a sugar-plum than my time.' He confesses 'a tendency to class women in my books with roses and sweetmeats—they never see themselves dominant'; and he can understand how the unpopularity of his poems may be in part due to 'the offence which the ladies,' not unnaturally 'take at him' from this cause. Even to Fanny Brawne he can write 'a flint-worded letter,' when his 'mind is heaped to the full' with poetry :—

'I know the generality of women would hate me for this ; that I should have so unsoftened, so hard a mind as to forget them ; forget the brightest realities for the dull imaginations of my own brain. . . . My heart seems now made of iron—I could not write a proper answer to an invitation to Idalia.'

The truth is that 'the yearning passion for the Beautiful,' which was with Keats, as he himself truly says, the master-passion, is not a passion of the sensuous or sentimental man, is not a passion of the sensuous or sentimental poet. It is an intellectual and spiritual passion. It is 'connected and made one,' as Keats declares that in his case

it was, 'with the ambition of the intellect.' It is,
as he again says, 'the mighty *abstract idea* of
Beauty in all things.' And in his last days Keats
wrote : 'If I should die, I have left no immortal
work behind me—nothing to make my friends
proud of my memory ; *but I have loved the principle of beauty in all things*, and if I had had time
I would have made myself remembered.' He *has*
made himself remembered, and remembered as no
merely sensuous poet could be ; and he has done
it by having 'loved the principle of beauty in all
things.'

For to see things in their beauty is to see
things in their truth, and Keats knew it. 'What
the Imagination seizes as Beauty must be Truth,'
he says in prose ; and in immortal verse he has
said the same thing—

> 'Beauty is truth, truth beauty,—that is all
> Ye know on earth, and all ye need to know.'

No, it is not all ; but it is true, deeply true, and
we have deep need to know it. And with beauty
goes not only truth, joy goes with her also ; and

this too Keats saw and said, as in the famous first
line of his *Endymion* it stands written—

     'A thing of beauty is a joy for ever.'

It is no small thing to have so loved the
principle of beauty as to perceive the necessary
relation of beauty with truth, and of both with
joy. Keats was a great spirit, and counts for far
more than many even of his admirers suppose,
because this just and high perception made itself
clear to him. Therefore a dignity and a glory
shed gleams over his life, and happiness, too, was
not a stranger to it. 'Nothing startles me beyond
the moment,' he says; 'the setting sun will always
set me to rights, or if a sparrow come before my
window I take part in its existence and pick about
the gravel.' But he had terrible bafflers,—con-
suming disease and early death. 'I think,' he
writes to Reynolds, 'if I had a free and healthy
and lasting organisation of heart, and lungs as
strong as an ox's, so as to be able to bear unhurt
the shock of extreme thought and sensation with-

out weariness, I could pass my life very nearly
alone, though it should last eighty years.   But
I feel my body too weak to support me to the
height; I am obliged continually to check myself,
and be nothing.'   He had against him even more
than this ; he had against him the blind power
which we call Fortune.   'O that something for-
tunate,' he cries in the closing months of his life,
' had ever happened to me or my brothers !—then
I might hope,—but despair is forced upon me as
a habit.'   So baffled and so sorely tried, — while
laden, at the same time, with a mighty formative
thought requiring health, and many days, and
favouring circumstances, for its adequate manifestation, — what wonder if the achievement of
Keats be partial and incomplete ?

Nevertheless, let and hindered as he was, and
with a short term and imperfect experience,—
'young,' as he says of himself, 'and writing at
random, straining after particles of light in the
midst of a great darkness, without knowing the
bearing of any one assertion, of any one opinion,'

—notwithstanding all this, by virtue of his feeling
for beauty and of his perception of the vital connection of beauty with truth, Keats accomplished
so much in poetry, that in one of the two great
modes by which poetry interprets, in the faculty
of naturalistic interpretation, in what we call
natural magic, he ranks with Shakespeare.   'The
tongue of Kean,' he says in an admirable criticism
of that great actor and of his enchanting elocution,
'the tongue of Kean must seem to have robbed
the Hybla bees and left them honeyless.   There is
an indescribable *gusto* in his voice ;—in *Richard*,
"Be stirring with the lark to-morrow, gentle Norfolk!" comes from him as through the morning
atmosphere towards which he yearns.'   This magic,
this 'indescribable *gusto* in the voice,' Keats himself, too, exhibits in his poetic expression.   No
one else in English poetry, save Shakespeare, has
in expression quite the fascinating felicity of Keats,
his perfection of loveliness.   'I think,' he said
humbly, 'I shall be among the English poets after
my death.'   He is; he is with Shakespeare.

For the second great half of poetic interpretation, for that faculty of moral interpretation which
is in Shakespeare, and is informed by him with
the same power of beauty as his naturalistic interpretation, Keats was not ripe. For the architectonics of poetry, the faculty which presides at
the evolution of works like the *Agamemnon* or
Lear, he was not ripe. His *Endymion*, as he
himself well saw, is a failure, and his *Hyperion*,
fine things as it contains, is not a success. But
in shorter things, where the matured power of
moral interpretation, and the high architectonics
which go with complete poetic development, are
not required, he is perfect. The poems which
follow prove it,—prove it far better by themselves
than anything which can be said about them will
prove it. Therefore I have chiefly spoken here of
the man, and of the elements in him which explain
the production of such work. Shakespearian work
it is ; not imitative, indeed, of Shakespeare, but
Shakespearian, because its expression has that
rounded perfection and felicity of loveliness of

which Shakespeare is the great master.   To show
such work is to praise it.   Let us now end by
delighting ourselves with a fragment of it, too
broken to find a place among the pieces which
follow, but far too beautiful to be lost.   It is a
fragment of an ode for May-day.   O might I, he
cries to May, O might I

'. . . thy smiles

Seek as they once were sought, in Grecian isles,
By bards who died content on pleasant sward,
Leaving great verse unto a little clan !
O, give me their old vigour, and unheard
Save of the quiet primrose, and the span
        Of heaven, and few years,
Rounded by thee, my song should die away,
        Content as theirs,
Rich in the simple worship of a day !'

V

WORDSWORTH[1]

I REMEMBER hearing Lord Macaulay say, after
Wordsworth's death, when subscriptions were
being collected to found a memorial of him, that
ten years earlier more money could have been
raised in Cambridge alone, to do honour to Wordsworth, than was now raised all through the
country. Lord Macaulay had, as we know, his
own heightened and telling way of putting things,
and we must always make allowance for it. But
probably it is true that Wordsworth has never,
either before or since, been so accepted and
popular, so established in possession of the minds
of all who profess to care for poetry, as he was

[1] The preface to *The Poems of Wordsworth*, chosen and
edited by Matthew Arnold, 1879.

between the years 1830 and 1840, and at Cambridge. From the very first, no doubt, he had his believers and witnesses. But I have myself heard him declare that, for he knew not how many years, his poetry had never brought him in enough to buy his shoe-strings. The poetry-reading public was very slow to recognise him, and was very easily drawn away from him. Scott effaced him with this public, Byron effaced him.

The death of Byron, seemed, however, to make an opening for Wordsworth. Scott, who had for some time ceased to produce poetry himself, and stood before the public as a great novelist; Scott, too genuine himself not to feel the profound genuineness of Wordsworth, and with an instinctive recognition of his firm hold on nature and of his local truth, always admired him sincerely, and praised him generously. The influence of Coleridge upon young men of ability was then powerful, and was still gathering strength; this influence told entirely in favour of Wordsworth's poetry. Cambridge was a place where Coleridge's influence had great action, and where Wordsworth's poetry, therefore, flourished especially. But even amongst the general public its sale grew large, the eminence of its author was widely recognised, and Rydal Mount became an object of pilgrimage. I remember Wordsworth relating how one of the pilgrims, a clergyman, asked him if he had ever written anything besides the *Guide to the Lakes.* Yes, he answered modestly, he had written verses Not every pilgrim was a reader, but the vogue was established, and the stream of pilgrims came.

Mr. Tennyson's decisive appearance dates from 1842. One cannot say that he effaced Wordsworth as Scott and Byron had effaced him. The poetry of Wordsworth had been so long before the public, the suffrage of good judges was so steady and so strong in its favour, that by 1842 the verdict of posterity, one may almost say, had been already pronounced, and Wordsworth's English fame was secure. But the vogue, the ear and applause of the great body of poetry-readers, never quite thoroughly perhaps his, he gradually lost more and more, and Mr

Tennyson gained them. Mr. Tennyson drew to himself, and away from Wordsworth, the poetry-reading public, and the new generations. Even in 1850, when Wordsworth died, this diminution of popularity was visible, and occasioned the remark of Lord Macaulay which I quoted at starting.

The diminution has continued. The influence of Coleridge has waned, and Wordsworth's poetry can no longer draw succour from this ally. The poetry has not, however, wanted eulogists; and it may be said to have brought its eulogists luck, for almost every one who has praised Wordsworth's poetry has praised it well. But the public has remained cold, or, at least, undetermined. Even the abundance of Mr. Palgrave's fine and skilfully chosen specimens of Wordsworth, in the *Golden Treasury*, surprised many readers, and gave offence to not a few. To tenth-rate critics and compilers, for whom any violent shock to the public taste would be a temerity not to be risked, it is still quite permissible to speak of Wordsworth's poetry, not only with ignorance, but with impertinence. On the Continent he is almost unknown.

I cannot think, then, that Wordsworth has, up to this time, at all obtained his deserts. 'Glory,' said M. Renan the other day, 'glory after all is the thing which has the best chance of not being altogether vanity.' Wordsworth was a homely man, and himself would certainly never have thought of talking of glory as that which, after all, has the best chance of not being altogether vanity. Yet we may well allow that few things are less vain than *real* glory. Let us conceive of the whole group of civilised nations as being, for intellectual and spiritual purposes, one great confederation, bound to a joint action and working towards a common result ; a confederation whose members have a due knowledge both of the past, out of which they all proceed, and of one another. This was the ideal of Goethe, and it is an ideal which will impose itself upon the thoughts of our modern societies more and more. Then to be recognised by the verdict of such a confederation as a master,

or even as a seriously and eminently worthy workman, in one's own line of intellectual or spiritual
activity, is indeed glory; a glory which it would
be difficult to rate too highly. For what could be
more beneficent, more salutary? The world is
forwarded by having its attention fixed on the
best things; and here is a tribunal, free from all
suspicion of national and provincial partiality,
putting a stamp on the best things, and recommending them for general honour and acceptance.
A nation, again, is furthered by recognition of its
real gifts and successes; it is encouraged to develop
them further. And here is an honest verdict, telling us which of our supposed successes are really,
in the judgment of the great impartial world, and
not in our own private judgment only, successes,
and which are not.

It is so easy to feel pride and satisfaction in
one's own things, so hard to make sure that one is
right in feeling it! We have a great empire.
But so had Nebuchadnezzar. We extol the 'un-
rivalled happiness' of our national civilisation.

But then comes a candid friend, and remarks that our upper class is materialised, our middle class vulgarised, and our lower class brutalised. We are proud of our painting, our music. But we find that in the judgment of other people our painting is questionable, and our music non-existent. We are proud of our men of science. And here it turns out that the world is with us; we find that in the judgment of other people, too, Newton among the dead, and Mr. Darwin among the living, hold as high a place as they hold in our national opinion.

Finally, we are proud of our poets and poetry. Now poetry is nothing less than the most perfect speech of man, that in which he comes nearest to being able to utter the truth. It is no small thing, therefore, to succeed eminently in poetry. And so much is required for duly estimating success here, that about poetry it is perhaps hardest to arrive at a sure general verdict, and takes longest. Meanwhile, our own conviction of the superiority of our national poets is not decisive, is almost certain to be mingled, as we see constantly in English eulogy of Shakespeare, with much of provincial infatuation. And we know what was the opinion current amongst our neighbours the French—people of taste, acuteness, and quick literary tact—not a hundred years ago, about our great poets. The old *Biographie Universelle* notices the pretension of the English to a place for their poets among the chief poets of the world, and says that this is a pretension which to no one but an Englishman can ever seem admissible. And the scornful, disparaging things said by foreigners about Shakespeare and Milton, and about our national over-estimate of them, have been often quoted, and will be in every one's remembrance.

A great change has taken place, and Shakespeare is now generally recognised, even in France, as one of the greatest of poets. Yes, some anti-Gallican cynic will say, the French rank him with Corneille and with Victor Hugo! But let me have the pleasure of quoting a sentence about Shakespeare, which I met with by accident not long ago in the *Correspondant*, a French review

which not a dozen English people, I suppose, look
at. The writer is praising Shakespeare's prose.
With Shakespeare, he says, ' prose comes in whenever the subject, being more familiar, is unsuited
to the majestic English iambic.' And he goes
on : ' Shakespeare is the king of poetic rhythm
and style, as well as the king of the realm of
thought ; along with his dazzling prose, Shakespeare has succeeded in giving us the most varied,
the most harmonious verse which has ever sounded
upon the human ear since the verse of the Greeks.'
M. Henry Cochin, the writer of this sentence,
deserves our gratitude for it ; it would not be easy
to praise Shakespeare, in a single sentence, more
justly. And when a foreigner and a Frenchman
writes thus of Shakespeare, and when Goethe says
of Milton, in whom there was so much to repel
Goethe rather than to attract him, that ' nothing
has been ever done so entirely in the sense of the
Greeks as *Samson Agonistes*,' and that ' Milton is
in very truth a poet whom we must treat with all
reverence,' then we understand what constitutes

a European recognition of poets and poetry as contradistinguished from a merely national recognition, and that in favour both of Milton and of Shakespeare the judgment of the high court of appeal has finally gone.

I come back to M. Renan's praise of glory, from which I started. Yes, real glory is a most serious thing, glory authenticated by the Amphictyonic Court of final appeal, definitive glory. And even for poets and poetry, long and difficult as may be the process of arriving at the right award, the right award comes at last, the definitive glory rests where it is deserved. Every establishment of such a real glory is good and wholesome for mankind at large, good and wholesome for the nation which produced the poet crowned with it. To the poet himself it can seldom do harm; for he, poor man, is in his grave, probably, long before his glory crowns him.

Wordsworth has been in his grave for some thirty years, and certainly his lovers and admirers cannot flatter themselves that this great and

steady light of glory as yet shines over him. He
is not fully recognised at home ; he is not recognised at all abroad. Yet I firmly believe that the
poetical performance of Wordsworth is, after that
of Shakespeare and Milton, of which all the world
now recognises the worth, undoubtedly the most
considerable in our language from the Elizabethan
age to the present time. Chaucer is anterior ;
and on other grounds, too, he cannot well be
brought into the comparison. But taking the roll
of our chief poetical names, besides Shakespeare
and Milton, from the age of Elizabeth downwards,
and going through it,—Spenser, Dryden, Pope,
Gray, Goldsmith, Cowper, Burns, Coleridge, Scott,
Campbell, Moore, Byron, Shelley, Keats (I mention those only who are dead),—I think it certain
that Wordsworth's name deserves to stand, and
will finally stand, above them all. Several of the
poets named have gifts and excellences which
Wordsworth has not. But taking the performance
of each as a whole, I say that Wordsworth seems
to me to have left a body of poetical work superior

in power, in interest, in the qualities which give
enduring freshness, to that which any one of the
others has left.

But this is not enough to say. I think it certain, further, that if we take the chief poetical
names of the Continent since the death of Molière,
and, omitting Goethe, confront the remaining
names with that of Wordsworth, the result is the
same. Let us take Klopstock, Lessing, Schiller,
Uhland, Rückert, and Heine for Germany ; Fili-
caia, Alfieri, Manzoni, and Leopardi for Italy ;
Racine, Boileau, Voltaire, André Chenier, Béranger, Lamartine, Musset, M. Victor Hugo (he
has been so long celebrated that although he still
lives I may be permitted to name him) for France.
Several of these, again, have evidently gifts and
excellences to which Wordsworth can make no
pretension. But in real poetical achievement it
seems to me indubitable that to Wordsworth, here
again, belongs the palm. It seems to me that
Wordsworth has left behind him a body of poetical work which wears, and will wear, better on

the whole than the performance of any one of these personages, so far more brilliant and celebrated, most of them, than the homely poet of Rydal. Wordsworth's performance in poetry is on the whole, in power, in interest, in the qualities which give enduring freshness, superior to theirs.

This is a high claim to make for Wordsworth. But if it is a just claim, if Wordsworth's place among the poets who have appeared in the last two or three centuries is after Shakespeare, Molière, Milton, Goethe, indeed, but before all the rest, then in time Wordsworth will have his due. We shall recognise him in his place, as we recognise Shakespeare and Milton ; and not only we ourselves shall recognise him, but he will be recognised by Europe also. Meanwhile, those who recognise him already may do well, perhaps, to ask themselves whether there are not in the case of Wordsworth certain special obstacles which hinder or delay his due recognition by others, and whether these obstacles are not in some measure removable.

The *Excursion* and the *Prelude,* his poems of greatest bulk, are by no means Wordsworth's best work. His best work is in his shorter pieces, and many indeed are there of these which are of first-rate excellence. But in his seven volumes the pieces of high merit are mingled with a mass of pieces very inferior to them ; so inferior to them that it seems wonderful how the same poet should have produced both. Shakespeare frequently has lines and passages in a strain quite false, and which are entirely unworthy of him. But one can imagine his smiling if one could meet him in the Elysian Fields and tell him so ; smiling and replying that he knew it perfectly well himself, and what did it matter ? But with Wordsworth the case is different. Work altogether inferior, work quite uninspired, flat and dull, is produced by him with evident unconsciousness of its defects, and he presents it to us with the same faith and seriousness as his best work. Now a drama or an epic fill the mind, and one does not look beyond them ; but in a collection of short pieces the impression made by one piece requires to be continued and sustained by the piece following. In reading Wordsworth the impression made by one of his fine pieces is too often dulled and spoiled by a very inferior piece coming after it.

Wordsworth composed verses during a space of some sixty years; and it is no exaggeration to say that within one single decade of those years, between 1798 and 1808, almost all his really first-rate work was produced. A mass of inferior work remains, work done before and after this golden prime, imbedding the first-rate work and clogging it, obstructing our approach to it, chilling, not unfrequently, the high-wrought mood with which we leave it. To be recognised far and wide as a great poet, to be possible and receivable as a classic, Wordsworth needs to be relieved of a great deal of the poetical baggage which now encumbers him. To administer this relief is indispensable, unless he is to continue to be a poet for the few only,—a poet valued far below his real worth by the world.

There is another thing. Wordsworth classified
his poems not according to any commonly received
plan of arrangement, but according to a scheme of
mental physiology. He has poems of the fancy,
poems of the imagination, poems of sentiment and
reflection, and so on. His categories are ingenious
but far-fetched, and the result of his employment
of them is unsatisfactory. Poems are separated
one from another which possess a kinship of
subject or of treatment far more vital and deep
than the supposed unity of mental origin, which
was Wordsworth's reason for joining them with
others.

The tact of the Greeks in matters of this kind
was infallible. We may rely upon it that we
shall not improve upon the classification adopted
by the Greeks for kinds of poetry ; that their
categories of epic, dramatic, lyric, and so forth,
have a natural propriety, and should be adhered
to. It may sometimes seem doubtful to which of
two categories a poem belongs ; whether this or
that poem is to be called, for instance, narrative

or lyric, lyric or elegiac.   But there is to be found
in every good poem a strain, a predominant note,
which determines the poem as belonging to one of
these kinds rather than the other ; and here is
the best proof of the value of the classification,
and of the advantage of adhering to it.   Wordsworth's poems will never produce their due effect
until they are freed from their present artificial
arrangement, and grouped more naturally.

Disengaged from the quantity of inferior work
which now obscures them, the best poems of
Wordsworth, I hear many people say, would
indeed stand out in great beauty, but they would
prove to be very few in number, scarcely more
than half a dozen.   I maintain, on the other hand,
that what strikes me with admiration, what establishes in my opinion Wordsworth's superiority,
is the great and ample body of powerful work
which remains to him, even after all his inferior
work has been cleared away.   He gives us so
much to rest upon, so much which communicates
his spirit and engages ours !

This is of very great importance. If it were a comparison of single pieces, or of three or four pieces, by each poet, I do not say that Wordsworth would stand decisively above Gray, or Burns, or Coleridge, or Keats, or Manzoni, or Heine. It is in his ampler body of powerful work that I find his superiority. His good work itself, his work which counts, is not all of it, of course, of equal value. Some kinds of poetry are in themselves lower kinds than others. The ballad kind is a lower kind; the didactic kind, still more, is a lower kind. Poetry of this latter sort counts, too, sometimes, by its biographical interest partly, not by its poetical interest pure and simple; but then this can only be when the poet producing it has the power and importance of Wordsworth, a power and importance which he assuredly did not establish by such didactic poetry alone. Altogether, it is, I say, by the great body of powerful and significant work which remains to him, after every reduction and deduction has been made, that Wordsworth's superiority is proved.

To exhibit this body of Wordsworth's best work, to clear away obstructions from around it, and to let it speak for itself, is what every lover of Wordsworth should desire. Until this has been done, Wordsworth, whom we, to whom he is dear, all of us know and feel to be so great a poet, has not had a fair chance before the world. When once it has been done, he will make his way best, not by our advocacy of him, but by his own worth and power. We may safely leave him to make his way thus, we who believe that a superior worth and power in poetry finds in mankind a sense responsive to it and disposed at last to recognise it. Yet at the outset, before he has been duly known and recognised, we may do Wordsworth a service, perhaps, by indicating in what his superior power and worth will be found to consist, and in what it will not.

Long ago, in speaking of Homer, I said that the noble and profound application of ideas to life is the most essential part of poetic greatness. I said that a great poet receives his distinctive character of superiority from his application, under the conditions immutably fixed by the laws of poetic beauty and poetic truth, from his application, I say, to his subject, whatever it may be, of the ideas

'On man, on nature, and on human life,'

which he has acquired for himself. The line quoted is Wordsworth's own; and his superiority arises from his powerful use, in his best pieces, his powerful application to his subject, of ideas 'on man, on nature, and on human life.'

Voltaire, with his signal acuteness, most truly remarked that 'no nation has treated in poetry moral ideas with more energy and depth than the English nation.' And he adds: 'There, it seems to me, is the great merit of the English poets.' Voltaire does not mean, by 'treating in poetry moral ideas,' the composing moral and didactic poems;—that brings us but a very little way in poetry. He means just the same thing as was meant when I spoke above 'of the noble and pro-

found application of ideas to life'; and he means
the application of these ideas under the conditions
fixed for us by the laws of poetic beauty and
poetic truth.   If it is said that to call these ideas
moral ideas is to introduce a strong and injurious
limitation, I answer that it is to do nothing of the
kind, because moral ideas are really so main a
part of human life.   The question, *how to live*, is
itself a moral idea; and it is the question which
most interests every man, and with which, in
some way or other, he is perpetually occupied.
A large sense is of course to be given to the
term *moral*.   Whatever bears upon the question,
'how to live,' comes under it.

> 'Nor love thy life, nor hate; but, what thou liv'st,
> Live well; how long or short, permit to heaven.'

In those fine lines Milton utters, as every one at
once perceives, a moral idea.   Yes, but so too,
when Keats consoles the forward-bending lover
on the Grecian Urn, the lover arrested and presented in immortal relief by the sculptor's hand
before he can kiss, with the line,

'For ever wilt thou love, and she be fair'—

he utters a moral idea.   When Shakespeare says,
that

> 'We are such stuff
> As dreams are made of, and our little life
> Is rounded with a sleep,'

he utters a moral idea.

Voltaire was right in thinking that the energetic
and profound treatment of moral ideas, in this
large sense, is what distinguishes the English
poetry.   He sincerely meant praise, not dispraise
or hint of limitation; and they err who suppose
that poetic limitation is a necessary consequence
of the fact, the fact being granted as Voltaire
states it.   If what distinguishes the greatest poets
is their powerful and profound application of ideas
to life, which surely no good critic will deny, then
to prefix to the term ideas here the term moral
makes hardly any difference, because human life
itself is in so preponderating a degree moral.

It is important, therefore, to hold fast to this:
that poetry is at bottom a criticism of life; that

the greatness of a poet lies in his powerful and beautiful application of ideas to life,—to the question : How to live. Morals are often treated in a narrow and false fashion ; they are bound up with systems of thought and belief which have had their day ; they are fallen into the hands of pedants and professional dealers; they grow tiresome to some of us. We find attraction, at times, even in a poetry of revolt against them ; in a poetry which might take for its motto Omar Kheyam's words : ' Let us make up in the tavern for the time which we have wasted in the mosque.' Or we find attractions in a poetry indifferent to them ; in a poetry where the contents may be what they will, but where the form is studied and exquisite. We delude ourselves in either case ; and the best cure for our delusion is to let our minds rest upon that great and inexhaustible word *life*, until we learn to enter into its meaning. A poetry of revolt against moral ideas is a poetry of revolt against *life* ; a poetry of indifference towards moral ideas is a poetry of indifference towards *life*.

Epictetus had a happy figure for things like the play of the senses, or literary form and finish, or argumentative ingenuity, in comparison with 'the best and master thing' for us, as he called it, the concern, how to live. Some people were afraid of them, he said, or they disliked and undervalued them. Such people were wrong; they were unthankful or cowardly. But the things might also be over-prized, and treated as final when they are not. They bear to life the relation which inns bear to home. 'As if a man, journeying home, and finding a nice inn on the road, and liking it, were to stay for ever at the inn! Man, thou hast forgotten thine object; thy journey was not *to* this, but *through* this. "But this inn is taking." And how many other inns, too, are taking, and how many fields and meadows! but as places of passage merely. You have an object, which is this: to get home, to do your duty to your family, friends, and fellow-countrymen, to attain inward freedom, serenity, happiness, contentment. Style takes your fancy, arguing takes your fancy,

L

and you forget your home and want to make your
abode with them and to stay with them, on the plea
that they are taking.   Who denies that they are
taking? but as places of passage, as inns.   And
when I say this, you suppose me to be attacking
the care for style, the care for argument.   I am
not ; I attack the resting in them, the not looking
to the end which is beyond them.'

Now, when we come across a poet like Théo-
phile Gautier, we have a poet who has taken up
his abode at an inn, and never got farther.   There
may be inducements to this or that one of us, at this
or that moment, to find delight in him, to cleave to
him ; but after all, we do not change the truth
about him,—we only stay ourselves in his inn
along with him.   And when we come across a
poet like Wordsworth, who sings

' Of truth, of grandeur, beauty, love and hope.
  And melancholy fear subdued by faith,
  Of blessed consolations in distress,
  Of moral strength and intellectual power,
  Of joy in widest commonalty spread '—

then we have a poet intent on ' the best and

master thing,' and who prosecutes his journey
home. We say, for brevity's sake, that he deals
with *life*, because he deals with that in which life
really consists. This is what Voltaire means to
praise in the English poets,—this dealing with
what is really life. But always it is the mark of
the greatest poets that they deal with it ; and to
say that the English poets are remarkable for
dealing with it, is only another way of saying,
what is true, that in poetry the English genius
has especially shown its power.

Wordsworth deals with it, and his greatness
lies in his dealing with it so powerfully. I have
named a number of celebrated poets above all of
whom he, in my opinion, deserves to be placed.
He is to be placed above poets like Voltaire, Dryden, Pope, Lessing, Schiller, because these famous
personages, with a thousand gifts and merits,
never, or scarcely ever, attain the distinctive accent and utterance of the high and genuine poets—

'Quique pii vates et Phœbo digna locuti,'

at all. Burns, Keats, Heine, not to speak of

others in our list, have this accent;—who can doubt it? And at the same time they have treasures of humour, felicity, passion, for which in Wordsworth we shall look in vain. Where, then, is Wordsworth's superiority? It is here; he deals with more of *life* than they do; he deals with *life*, as a whole, more powerfully.

No Wordsworthian will doubt this. Nay, the fervent Wordsworthian will add, as Mr. Leslie Stephen does, that Wordsworth's poetry is precious because his philosophy is sound ; that his ' ethical system is as distinctive and capable of exposition as Bishop Butler's ' ; that his poetry is informed by ideas which ' fall spontaneously into a scientific system of thought.' But we must be on our guard against the Wordsworthians, if we want to secure for Wordsworth his due rank as a poet. The Wordsworthians are apt to praise him for the wrong things, and to lay far too much stress upon what they call his philosophy. His poetry is the reality, his philosophy,—so far, at least, as it may put on the form and habit of ' a scientific system of thought,' and the more that it puts them on, —is the illusion. Perhaps we shall one day learn to make this proposition general, and to say: Poetry is the reality, philosophy the illusion. But in Wordsworth's case, at any rate, we cannot do him justice until we dismiss his formal philosophy.

The *Excursion* abounds with philosophy, and therefore the *Excursion* is to the Wordsworthian what it never can be to the disinterested lover of poetry,—a satisfactory work. 'Duty exists,' says Wordsworth, in the *Excursion ;* and then he proceeds thus—

> '. . . Immutably survive,
> For our support, the measures and the forms,
> Which an abstract Intelligence supplies,
> Whose kingdom is, where time and space are not.'

And the Wordsworthian is delighted, and thinks that here is a sweet union of philosophy and poetry. But the disinterested lover of poetry will feel that the lines carry us really not a step farther than the proposition which they would interpret;

that they are a tissue of elevated but abstract verbiage, alien to the very nature of poetry.

Or let us come direct to the centre of Wordsworth's philosophy, as 'an ethical system, as distinctive and capable of systematical exposition as Bishop Butler's'—

> '. . . One adequate support
> For the calamities of mortal life
> Exists, one only ;—an assured belief
> That the procession of our fate, howe'er
> Sad or disturbed, is ordered by a Being
> Of infinite benevolence and power ;
> Whose everlasting purposes embrace
> All accidents, converting them to good.'

That is doctrine such as we hear in church too, religious and philosophic doctrine ; and the attached Wordsworthian loves passages of such doctrine, and brings them forward in proof of his poet's excellence. But however true the doctrine may be, it has, as here presented, none of the characters of *poetic* truth, the kind of truth which we require from a poet, and in which Wordsworth is really strong.

Even the 'intimations' of the famous Ode, those corner-stones of the supposed philosophic system of Wordsworth,—the idea of the high instincts and affections coming out in childhood, testifying of a divine home recently left, and fading away as our life proceeds,—this idea, of undeniable beauty as a play of fancy, has itself not the character of poetic truth of the best kind; it has no real solidity. The instinct of delight in Nature and her beauty had no doubt extraordinary strength in Wordsworth himself as a child. But to say that universally this instinct is mighty in childhood, and tends to die away afterwards, is to say what is extremely doubtful. In many people, perhaps with the majority of educated persons, the love of nature is nearly imperceptible at ten years old, but strong and operative at thirty. In general we may say of these high instincts of early childhood, the base of the alleged systematic philosophy of Wordsworth, what Thucydides says of the early achievements of the Greek race: 'It is impossible to speak with certainty of what is so remote ; but from all that we can really investigate, I should say that they were no very great things.'

Finally, the ' scientific system of thought ' in Wordsworth gives us at last such poetry as this, which the devout Wordsworthian accepts—

' O for the coming of that glorious time
When, prizing knowledge as her noblest wealth
And best protection, this Imperial Realm,
While she exacts allegiance, shall admit
An obligation, on her part, to *teach*
Them who are born to serve her and obey ;
Binding herself by statute to secure,
For all the children whom her soil maintains,
The rudiments of letters, and inform
The mind with moral and religious truth.'

Wordsworth calls Voltaire dull, and surely the production of these un-Voltairian lines must have been imposed on him as a judgment! One can hear them being quoted at a Social Science Congress ; one can call up the whole scene. A great room in one of our dismal provincial towns ; dusty air and jaded afternoon daylight ; benches full of men with bald heads and women in spectacles ;

an orator lifting up his face from a manuscript written within and without to declaim these lines of Wordsworth; and in the soul of any poor child of nature who may have wandered in thither, an unutterable sense of lamentation, and mourning, and woe!

'But turn we,' as Wordsworth says, 'from these bold, bad men,' the haunters of Social Science Congresses. And let us be on our guard, too, against the exhibitors and extollers of a 'scientific system of thought' in Wordsworth's poetry. The poetry will never be seen aright while they thus exhibit it. The cause of its greatness is simple, and may be told quite simply. Wordsworth's poetry is great because of the extraordinary power with which Wordsworth feels the joy offered to us in nature, the joy offered to us in the simple primary affections and duties; and because of the extraordinary power with which, in case after case, he shows us this joy, and renders it so as to make us share it.

The source of joy from which he thus draws is

the truest and most unfailing source of joy accessible to man. It is also accessible universally. Wordsworth brings us word, therefore, according to his own strong and characteristic line, he brings us word

  ' Of joy in widest commonalty spread.'

Here is an immense advantage for a poet. Wordsworth tells of what all seek, and tells of it at its truest and best source, and yet a source where all may go and draw for it.

  Nevertheless, we are not to suppose that everything is precious which Wordsworth, standing even at this perennial and beautiful source, may give us. Wordsworthians are apt to talk as if it must be. They will speak with the same reverence of *The Sailor's Mother*, for example, as of *Lucy Gray*. They do their master harm by such lack of discrimination. *Lucy Gray* is a beautiful success; *The Sailor's Mother* is a failure. To give aright what he wishes to give, to interpret and render successfully, is not always within Words-

worth's own command. It is within no poet's
command; here is the part of the Muse, the inspiration, the God, the 'not ourselves.' In Wordsworth's case, the accident, for so it may almost be
called, of inspiration, is of peculiar importance.
No poet, perhaps, is so evidently filled with a new
and sacred energy when the inspiration is upon
him; no poet, when it fails him, is so left ' weak
as is a breaking wave.' I remember hearing him
say that ' Goethe's poetry was not inevitable
enough.' The remark is striking and true; no
line in Goethe, as Goethe said himself, but its
maker knew well how it came there. Wordsworth
is right, Goethe's poetry is not inevitable; not inevitable enough. But Wordsworth's poetry, when he
is at his best, is inevitable, as inevitable as Nature
herself. It might seem that Nature not only gave
him the matter for his poem, but wrote his poem
for him. He has no style. He was too conversant
with Milton not to catch at times his master's
manner, and he has fine Miltonic lines; but he
has no assured poetic style of his own, like Milton

When he seeks to have a style he falls into ponderosity and pomposity. In the *Excursion* we have his style, as an artistic product of his own creation; and although Jeffrey completely failed to recognise Wordsworth's real greatness, he was yet not wrong in saying of the *Excursion*, as a work of poetic style : 'This will never do.' And yet magical as is that power, which Wordsworth has not, of assured and possessed poetic style, he has something which is an equivalent for it.

Every one who has any sense for these things feels the subtle turn, the heightening, which is given to a poet's verse by his genius for style. We can feel it in the

   ' After life's fitful fever, he sleeps well '—

of Shakespeare ; in the

   '. . . though fall'n on evil days,
On evil days though fall'n, and evil tongues '—

of Milton. It is the incomparable charm of Milton's power of poetic style which gives such worth to *Paradise Regained*, and makes a great

poem of a work in which Milton's imagination does
not soar high. Wordsworth has in constant possession, and at command, no style of this kind ; but
he had too poetic a nature, and had read the great
poets too well, not to catch, as I have already remarked, something of it occasionally. We find it not
only in his Miltonic lines; we find it in such a phrase
as this, where the manner is his own, not Milton's—

> '. . . the fierce confederate storm
> Of sorrow barricadoed evermore
> Within the walls of cities ;'

although even here, perhaps, the power of style
which is undeniable, is more properly that of eloquent prose than the subtle heightening and
change wrought by genuine poetic style. It is style,
again, and the elevation given by style, which
chiefly makes the effectiveness of *Laodameia*. Still
the right sort of verse to choose from Wordsworth,
if we are to seize his true and most characteristic
form of expression, is a line like this from *Michael*—

> 'And never lifted up a single stone.'

There is nothing subtle in it, no heightening, no

study of poetic style, strictly so called, at all ; yet it is expression of the highest and most truly expressive kind.

Wordsworth owed much to Burns, and a style of perfect plainness, relying for effect solely on the weight and force of that which with entire fidelity it utters, Burns could show him.

> ' The poor inhabitant below
>   Was quick to learn and wise to know,
>   And keenly felt the friendly glow
>   And softer flame ;
>   But thoughtless follies laid him low
>   And stain'd his name.'

Every one will be conscious of a likeness here to Wordsworth ; and if Wordsworth did great things with this nobly plain manner, we must remember, what indeed he himself would always have been forward to acknowledge, that Burns used it before him.

Still Wordsworth's use of it has something unique and unmatchable. Nature herself seems, I say, to take the pen out of his hand, and to write for him with her own bare, sheer, penetrating power. This arises from two causes ; from the profound sincereness with which Wordsworth feels his subject, and also from the profoundly sincere and natural character of his subject itself. He can and will treat such a subject with nothing but the most plain, first-hand, almost austere naturalness. His expression may often be called bald, as, for instance, in the poem of *Resolution and Independence;* but it is bald as the bare mountain tops are bald, with a baldness which is full of grandeur.

Wherever we meet with the successful balance, in Wordsworth, of profound truth of subject with profound truth of execution, he is unique. His best poems are those which most perfectly exhibit this balance. I have a warm admiration for *Laodameia* and for the great *Ode;* but if I am to tell the very truth, I find *Laodameia* not wholly free from something artificial, and the great *Ode* not wholly free from something declamatory. If I had to pick out poems of a kind most perfectly to show Wordsworth's unique power, I should rather choose poems such as *Michael, The Fountain, The Highland Reaper.* And poems with the peculiar and unique beauty which distinguishes these, Wordsworth produced in considerable number ; besides very many other poems of which the worth, although not so rare as the worth of these, is still exceedingly high.

On the whole, then, as I said at the beginning, not only is Wordsworth eminent by reason of the goodness of his best work, but he is eminent also by reason of the great body of good work which he has left to us. With the ancients I will not compare him. In many respects the ancients are far above us, and yet there is something that we demand which they can never give. Leaving the ancients, let us come to the poets and poetry of Christendom. Dante, Shakespeare, Molière, Milton, Goethe, are altogether larger and more splendid luminaries in the poetical heaven than Wordsworth. But I know not where else, among the moderns, we are to find his superiors.

To disengage the poems which show his power,

and to present them to the English-speaking public and to the world, is the object of this volume. I by no means say that it contains all which in Wordsworth's poems is interesting. Except in the case of *Margaret*, a story composed separately from the rest of the *Excursion*, and which belongs to a different part of England, I have not ventured on detaching portions of poems, or on giving any piece otherwise than as Wordsworth himself gave it. But under the conditions imposed by this reserve, the volume contains, I think, everything, or nearly everything, which may best serve him with the majority of lovers of poetry, nothing which may disserve him.

I have spoken lightly of Wordsworthians; and if we are to get Wordsworth recognised by the public and by the world, we must recommend him not in the spirit of a clique, but in the spirit of disinterested lovers of poetry. But I am a Wordsworthian myself. I can read with pleasure and edification *Peter Bell*, and the whole series of *Ecclesiastical Sonnets*, and the address to Mr. Wil-

kinson's spade, and even the *Thanksgiving Ode ;*—
everything of Wordsworth, I think, except *Vaud-
racour and Julia.* It is not for nothing that one
has been brought up in the veneration of a man so
truly worthy of homage; that one has seen him
and heard him, lived in his neighbourhood, and
been familiar with his country. No Wordsworthian has a tenderer affection for this pure and
sage master than I, or is less really offended by
his defects. But Wordsworth is something more
than the pure and sage master of a small band of
devoted followers, and we ought not to rest satisfied until he is seen to be what he is. He is one
of the very chief glories of English Poetry ; and by
nothing is England so glorious as by her poetry. Let
us lay aside every weight which hinders our getting
him recognised as this, and let our one study be to
bring to pass, as widely as possible and as truly as
possible, his own word concerning his poems :
' They will co-operate with the benign tendencies in
human nature and society, and will, in their degree, be
efficacious in making men wiser, better, and happier.'

BYRON[1]

WHEN at last I held in my hand the volume of poems which I had chosen from Wordsworth, and began to turn over its pages, there arose in me almost immediately the desire to see beside it, as a companion volume, a like collection of the best poetry of Byron. Alone amongst our poets of the earlier part of this century, Byron and Wordsworth not only furnish material enough for a volume of this kind, but also, as it seems to me, they both of them gain considerably by being thus exhibited. There are poems of Coleridge and of Keats equal, if not superior, to anything of Byron or Wordsworth; but a dozen pages or two will

[1] Preface to *Poetry of Byron*, chosen and arranged by Matthew Arnold, 1881.

contain them, and the remaining poetry is of a quality much inferior. Scott never, I think, rises as a poet to the level of Byron and Wordsworth at all. On the other hand, he never falls below his own usual level very far; and by a volume of selections from him, therefore, his effectiveness is not increased. As to Shelley there will be more question; and indeed Mr. Stopford Brooke, whose accomplishments, eloquence, and love of poetry we must all recognise and admire, has actually given us Shelley in such a volume. But for my own part I cannot think that Shelley's poetry, except by snatches and fragments, has the value of the good work of Wordsworth and Byron ; or that it is possible for even Mr. Stopford Brooke to make up a volume of selections from him which, for real substance, power, and worth, can at all take rank with a like volume from Byron or Wordsworth.

Shelley knew quite well the difference between the achievement of such a poet as Byron and his own. He praises Byron too unreservedly, but he

sincerely felt, and he was right in feeling, that
Byron was a greater poetical power than himself.
As a man, Shelley is at a number of points immeasurably Byron's superior; he is a beautiful
and enchanting spirit, whose vision, when we call
it up, has far more loveliness, more charm for our
soul, than the vision of Byron. But all the personal charm of Shelley cannot hinder us from at
last discovering in his poetry the incurable want,
in general, of a sound subject-matter, and the incurable fault, in consequence, of unsubstantiality.
Those who extol him as the poet of clouds, the
poet of sunsets, are only saying that he did not, in
fact, lay hold upon the poet's right subject-matter;
and in honest truth, with all his charm of soul and
spirit, and with all his gift of musical diction and
movement, he never, or hardly ever, did. Except,
as I have said, for a few short things and single
stanzas, his original poetry is less satisfactory than
his translations, for in these the subject-matter
was found for him. Nay, I doubt whether his
delightful Essays and Letters, which deserve to be

far more read than they are now, will not resist
the wear and tear of time better, and finally come
to stand higher, than his poetry.

There remain to be considered Byron and
Wordsworth.   That Wordsworth affords good
material for a volume of selections, and that he
gains by having his poetry thus presented, is an
old belief of mine which led me lately to make up
a volume of poems chosen out of Wordsworth, and
to bring it before the public.   By its kind reception of the volume, the public seems to show itself
a partaker in my belief.   Now Byron also supplies plenty of material for a like volume, and he
too gains, I think, by being so presented.   Mr.
Swinburne urges, indeed, that 'Byron, who rarely
wrote anything either worthless or faultless, can
only be judged or appreciated in the mass ; the
greatest of his works was his whole work taken
together.'   It is quite true that Byron rarely wrote
anything either worthless or faultless ; it is quite
true also that in the appreciation of Byron's
power a sense of the amount and variety of his

work, defective though much of his work is, enters justly into our estimate. But although there may be little in Byron's poetry which can be pronounced either worthless or faultless, there are portions of it which are far higher in worth and far more free from fault than others. And although, again, the abundance and variety of his production is undoubtedly a proof of his power, yet I question whether by reading everything which he gives us we are so likely to acquire an admiring sense even of his variety and abundance, as by reading what he gives us at his happier moments. Varied and abundant he amply proves himself even by this taken alone. Receive him absolutely without omission or compression, follow his whole outpouring stanza by stanza and line by line from the very commencement to the very end, and he is capable of being tiresome.

Byron has told us himself that the *Giaour* 'is but a string of passages.' He has made full confession of his own negligence. 'No one,' says he, 'has done more through negligence to corrupt the language.' This accusation brought by himself against his poems is not just; but when he goes on to say of them, that 'their faults, whatever they may be, are those of negligence and not of labour,' he says what is perfectly true. '*Lara*,' he declares, 'I wrote while undressing after coming home from balls and masquerades, in the year of revelry, 1814. The *Bride* was written in four, the *Corsair* in ten days.' He calls this 'a humiliating confession, as it proves my own want of judgment in publishing, and the public's in reading, things which cannot have stamina for permanence.' Again he does his poems injustice; the producer of such poems could not but publish them, the public could not but read them. Nor could Byron have produced his work in any other fashion; his poetic work could not have first grown and matured in his own mind, and then come forth as an organic whole; Byron had not enough of the artist in him for this, nor enough of self-command. He wrote, as he truly tells us, to relieve himself, and he went on writing because he found the relief become indispensable. But it was inevitable that works so produced should be, in general, 'a string of passages,' poured out, as he describes them, with rapidity and excitement, and with new passages constantly suggesting themselves, and added while his work was going through the press. It is evident that we have here neither deliberate scientific construction, nor yet the instinctive artistic creation of poetic wholes; and that to take passages from work produced as Byron's was is a very different thing from taking passages out of the *Œdipus* or the *Tempest*, and deprives the poetry far less of its advantage.

Nay, it gives advantage to the poetry, instead of depriving it of any. Byron, I said, has not a great artist's profound and patient skill in combining an action or in developing a character,—a skill which we must watch and follow if we are to do justice to it. But he has a wonderful power of vividly conceiving a single incident, a single situation; of throwing himself upon it, grasping it as if it were real and he saw and felt it, and of

making us see and feel it too. The *Giaour* is, as
he truly called it, ' a string of passages,' not a
work moving by a deep internal law of development to a necessary end; and our total impression from it cannot but receive from this, its in-
herent defect, a certain dimness and indistinctness
But the incidents of the journey and death of
Hassan, in that poem, are conceived and presented
with a vividness not to be surpassed; and our
impression from them is correspondingly clear
and powerful. In *Lara*, again, there is no
adequate development either of the character
of the chief personage or of the action of
the poem; our total impression from the work is
a confused one. Yet such an incident as the dis-
posal of the slain Ezzelin's body passes before our
eyes as if we actually saw it. And in the same
way as these bursts of incident, bursts of sentiment also, living and vigorous, often occur in the
midst of poems which must be admitted to be but
weakly-conceived and loosely-combined wholes.
Byron cannot but be a gainer by having attention

concentrated upon what is vivid, powerful, effective in his work, and withdrawn from what is not so.

Byron, I say, cannot but be a gainer by this, just as Wordsworth is a gainer by a like proceeding. I esteem Wordsworth's poetry so highly, and the world, in my opinion, has done it such scant justice, that I could not rest satisfied until I had fulfilled, on Wordsworth's behalf, a long-cherished desire ;—had disengaged, to the best of my power, his good work from the inferior work joined with it, and had placed before the public the body of his good work by itself. To the poetry of Byron the world has ardently paid homage; full justice from his contemporaries, perhaps even more than justice, his torrent of poetry received. His poetry was admired, adored, 'with all its imperfections on its head,'—in spite of negligence, in spite of diffuseness, in spite of repetitions, in spite of whatever faults it possessed. His name is still great and brilliant. Nevertheless the hour of irresistible vogue has passed away for him ; even for Byron it could not but pass away. The time has come for him, as it comes for all poets, when he must take his real and permanent place, no longer depending upon the vogue of his own day and upon the enthusiasm of his contemporaries. Whatever we may think of him, we shall not be subjugated by him as they were; for, as he cannot be for us what he was for them, we cannot admire him so hotly and indiscriminately as they. His faults of negligence, of diffuseness, of repetition, his faults of whatever kind, we shall abundantly feel and unsparingly criticise; the mere interval of time between us and him makes disillusion of this kind inevitable. But how then will Byron stand, if we relieve him too, so far as we can, of the encumbrance of his inferior and weakest work, and if we bring before us his best and strongest work in one body together? That is the question which I, who can even remember the latter years of Byron's vogue, and have myself felt the expiring wave of that mighty influence, but who certainly also regard him, and have long regarded him, without illusion, cannot but ask myself, cannot but seek to answer. The present volume is an attempt to provide adequate data for answering it.

Byron has been over-praised, no doubt. 'Byron is one of our French superstitions,' says M. Edmond Scherer; but where has Byron not been a superstition? He pays now the penalty of this exaggerated worship. 'Alone among the English poets his contemporaries, Byron,' said M. Taine, '*atteint à la cîme*,—gets to the top of the poetic mountain.' But the idol that M. Taine had thus adored M. Scherer is almost for burning. 'In Byron,' he declares, 'there is a remarkable inability ever to lift himself into the region of real poetic art,—art impersonal and disinterested,—at all. He has fecundity, eloquence, wit, but even these qualities themselves are confined within somewhat narrow limits. He has treated hardly any subject but one,—himself; now the man, in Byron, is of a nature even less sincere than the poet. This beautiful and blighted being is at bottom a coxcomb. He posed all his life long.'

Our poet could not well meet with more severe

and unsympathetic criticism. However, the praise often given to Byron has been so exaggerated as to provoke, perhaps, a reaction in which he is unduly disparaged. 'As various in composition as Shakespeare himself, Lord Byron has embraced,' says Sir Walter Scott, 'every topic of human life, and sounded every string on the divine harp, from its slightest to its most powerful and heart-astounding tones.' It is not surprising that some one with a cool head should retaliate, on such provocation as this, by saying: 'He has treated hardly any subject but one, *himself.*' 'In the very grand and tremendous drama of *Cain,*' says Scott, 'Lord Byron has certainly matched Milton on his own ground.' And Lord Byron has done all this, Scott adds. 'while managing his pen with the careless and negligent ease of a man of quality.' Alas, 'managing his pen with the careless and negligent ease of a man of quality,' Byron wrote in his *Cain*——

'Souls that dare look the Omnipotent tyrant in
   His everlasting face, and tell him that
   His evil is not good;'

or he wrote—

'. . . And *thou* would'st go on aspiring
To the great double Mysteries! the *two Principles!*'[1]

One has only to repeat to oneself a line from
Paradise Lost in order to feel the difference.

Sainte-Beuve, speaking of that exquisite master
of language, the Italian poet Leopardi, remarks
how often we see the alliance, singular though it
may at first sight appear, of the poetical genius
with the genius for scholarship and philology.
Dante and Milton are instances which will occur
to every one's mind. Byron is so negligent in his
poetical style, he is often, to say the truth, so
slovenly, slipshod, and infelicitous, he is so little
haunted by the true artist's fine passion for the
correct use and consummate management of words,
that he may be described as having for this artistic
gift the insensibility of the barbarian ;—which is
perhaps only another and a less flattering way of
saying, with Scott, that he 'manages his pen with

[1] The italics are in the original.

the careless and negligent ease of a man of quality.
Just of a piece with the rhythm of

> 'Dare you await the event of a few minutes'
>   Deliberation ?'

or of

>   'All shall be void—
>   Destroy'd !'

is the diction of

>   'Which now is painful to these eyes,
>   Which have not seen the sun to rise;'

or of

>   '. . . there let him lay !'

or of the famous passage beginning

>   'He who hath bent him o'er the dead;'

with those trailing relatives, that crying grammatical solecism, that inextricable anacolouthon!
To class the work of the author of such things
with the work of the authors of such verse as

>   'In the dark backward and abysm of time'—

or as

>   'Presenting Thebes, or Pelops' line,
>   Or the tale of Troy divine'—

is ridiculous. Shakespeare and Milton, with their secret of consummate felicity in diction and movement, are of another and an altogether higher order from Byron, nay, for that matter, from Wordsworth also; from the author of such verse as

> 'Sol hath dropt into his harbour'—

or (if Mr. Ruskin pleases) as

> 'Parching summer hath no warrant'—

as from the author of

> 'All shall be void—
>   Destroy'd!'

With a poetical gift and a poetical performance of the very highest order, the slovenliness and tunelessness of much of Byron's production, the pompousness and ponderousness of much of Wordsworth's are incompatible. Let us admit this to the full.

Moreover, while we are hearkening to M. Scherer, and going along with him in his faultfinding, let us admit, too, that the man in Byron

is in many respects as unsatisfactory as the poet.
And, putting aside all direct moral criticism of
him, — with which we need not concern ourselves here,—we shall find that he is unsatisfactory
in the same way. Some of Byron's most crying
faults as a man,—his vulgarity, his affectation,—
are really akin to the faults of commonness, of
want of art, in his workmanship as a poet. The
ideal nature for the poet and artist is that of the
finely touched and finely gifted man, the εὐφυής of
the Greeks ; now, Byron's nature was in substance not that of the εὐφυής at all, but rather,
as I have said, of the barbarian. The want of
fine perception which made it possible for him to
formulate either the comparison between himself
and Rousseau, or his reason for getting Lord Dela-
warr excused from a 'licking' at Harrow, is
exactly what made possible for him also his
terrible dealings in, *An ye wool ; I have redde thee ;
Sunburn me ; Oons, and it is excellent well.* It is
exactly, again, what made possible for him his
precious dictum that Pope is a Greek temple, and

a string of other criticisms of the like force; it is exactly, in fine, what deteriorated the quality of his poetic production. If we think of a good representative of that finely touched and exquisitely gifted nature which is the ideal nature for the poet and artist,—if we think of Raphael, for instance, who truly is εὐφυής just as Byron is not,—we shall bring into clearer light the connection in Byron between the faults of the man and the faults of the poet. With Raphael's character Byron's sins of vulgarity and false criticism would have been impossible, just as with Raphael's art Byron's sins of common and bad workmanship.

Yes, all this is true, but it is not the whole truth about Byron nevertheless; very far from it. The severe criticism of M. Scherer by no means gives us the whole truth about Byron, and we have not yet got it in what has been added to that criticism here. The negative part of the true criticism of him we perhaps have; the positive part, by far the more important, we have not.

Byron's admirers appeal eagerly to foreign testimonies in his favour. Some of these testimonies
do not much move me; but one testimony there
is among them which will always carry, with me
at any rate, very great weight,—the testimony of
Goethe. Goethe's sayings about Byron were
uttered, it must however be remembered, at the
height of Byron's vogue, when that puissant and
splendid personality was exercising its full power
of attraction. In Goethe's own household there
was an atmosphere of glowing Byron-worship;
his daughter-in-law was a passionate admirer of
Byron, nay, she enjoyed and prized his poetry, as
did Tieck and so many others in Germany at that
time, much above the poetry of Goethe himself.
Instead of being irritated and rendered jealous by
this, a nature like Goethe's was inevitably led by
it to heighten, not lower, the note of his praise.
The Time-Spirit, or *Zeit-Geist*, he would himself
have said, was working just then for Byron. This
working of the *Zeit-Geist* in his favour was an
advantage added to Byron's other advantages, an

advantage of which he had a right to get the benefit. This is what Goethe would have thought and said to himself; and so he would have been led even to heighten somewhat his estimate of Byron, and to accentuate the emphasis of praise. Goethe speaking of Byron at that moment was not and could not be quite the same cool critic as Goethe speaking of Dante, or Molière, or Milton. This, I say, we ought to remember in reading Goethe's judgments on Byron and his poetry. Still, if we are careful to bear this in mind, and if we quote Goethe's praise correctly,—which is not always done by those who in this country quote it,—and if we add to it that great and due quali-fication added to it by Goethe himself,—which so far as I have seen has never yet been done by his quoters in this country at all,—then we shall have a judgment on Byron, which comes, I think, very near to the truth, and which may well command our adherence.

In his judicious and interesting Life of Byron, Professor Nichol quotes Goethe as saying that

Byron 'is undoubtedly to be regarded as the greatest genius of our century.' What Goethe did really say was ' the greatest *talent*,' not ' the greatest *genius*.' The difference is important, because, while talent gives the notion of power in a man's performance, genius gives rather the notion of felicity and perfection in it ; and this divine gift of consummate felicity by no means, as we have seen, belongs to Byron and to his poetry. Goethe said that Byron 'must unquestionably be regarded as the greatest talent of the century.'[1] He said of him moreover : ' The English may think of Byron what they please, but it is certain that they can point to no poet who is his like. He is different from all the rest, and in the main greater.' Here, again, Professor Nichol translates : ' They can show no (living) poet who is to be compared to him ;'— inserting the word *living*, I suppose, to prevent its being thought that Goethe would have ranked Byron, as a poet,

---

[1] ' Der ohne Frage als das grösste Talent des Jahrhunderts anzusehen ist.

above Shakespeare and Milton. But Goethe did
not use, or, I think, mean to imply, any limitation
such as is added by Professor Nichol. Goethe said
simply, and he meant to say, '*no* poet.' Only
the words which follow[1] ought not, I think, to
be rendered, 'who is to be compared to him,'
that is to say, '*who is his equal as a poet.*' They
mean rather, 'who may properly be compared with
him,' '*who is his parallel.*' And when Goethe said
that Byron was 'in the main greater' than all
the rest of the English poets, he was not so
much thinking of the strict rank, as poetry, of
Byron's production; he was thinking of that
wonderful personality of Byron which so enters
into his poetry, and which Goethe called 'a
personality such, for its eminence, as has never
been yet, and such as is not likely to come again.'
He was thinking of that 'daring, dash, and gran-
diosity,'[2] of Byron, which are indeed so splendid;

---

[1] 'Der ihm zu vergleichen wäre.'
[2] 'Byron's Kühnheit, Keckheit und Grandiositat, ist das
nicht alles bildend ?—Alles Grosse bildet, sobald wir es gewahr
werden.'

and which were, so Goethe maintained, of a character to do good, because 'everything great is formative,' and what is thus formative does us good.

The faults which went with this greatness, and which impaired Byron's poetical work, Goethe saw very well. He saw the constant state of warfare and combat, the 'negative and polemical working,' which makes Byron's poetry a poetry in which we can so little find rest; he saw the *Hang zum Unbegrenzten,* the straining after the unlimited, which made it impossible for Byron to produce poetic wholes such as the *Tempest* or *Lear;* he saw the *zu viel Empirie,* the promiscuous adoption of all the matter offered to the poet by life, just as it was offered, without thought or patience for the mysterious transmutation to be operated on this matter by poetic form. But in a sentence which I cannot, as I say, remember to have yet seen quoted in any English criticism of Byron, Goethe lays his finger on the cause of all these defects in Byron, and on his real source of weakness both as a man and as a poet. 'The moment he reflects, he is a child,' says Goethe ;—'*sobald er reflectirt ist er ein Kind.*'

Now if we take the two parts of Goethe's criticism of Byron, the favourable and the unfavourable, and put them together, we shall have, I think, the truth. On the one hand, a splendid and puissant personality—a personality 'in eminence such as has never been yet, and is not likely to come again'; of which the like, therefore, is not to be found among the poets of our nation, by which Byron 'is different from all the rest, and in the main greater.' Byron is, moreover, 'the greatest talent of our century.' On the other hand, this splendid personality and unmatched talent, this unique Byron, 'is quite too much in the dark about himself;'[1] nay, 'the moment he begins to reflect, he is a child.' There we have, I think, Byron complete; and in estimating him and ranking him we have to strike a balance between the gain which accrues to his poetry, as

[1] 'Gar zu dunkel über sich selbst.'

compared with the productions of other poets, from his superiority, and the loss which accrues to it from his defects.

A balance of this kind has to be struck in the case of all poets except the few supreme masters in whom a profound criticism of life exhibits itself in indissoluble connection with the laws of poetic truth and beauty. I have seen it said that I allege poetry to have for its characteristic this: that it is a criticism of life; and that I make it to be thereby distinguished from prose, which is something else. So far from it, that when I first used this expression, *a criticism of life*, now many years ago, it was to literature in general that I applied it, and not to poetry in especial. 'The end and aim of all literature,' I said, 'is, if one considers it attentively, nothing but that: *a criticism of life*.' And so it surely is; the main end and aim of all our utterance, whether in prose or in verse, is surely a criticism of life. We are not brought much on our way, I admit, towards an adequate definition of poetry as distinguished from prose by that truth; still a truth it is, and poetry can never prosper if it is forgotten. In poetry, however, the criticism of life has to be made conformably to the laws of poetic truth and poetic beauty. Truth and seriousness of substance and matter, felicity and perfection of diction and manner, as these are exhibited in the best poets, are what constitute a criticism of life made in conformity with the laws of poetic truth and poetic beauty; and it is by knowing and feeling the work of those poets, that we learn to recognise the fulfilment and non-fulfilment of such conditions.

The moment, however, that we leave the small band of the very best poets, the true classics, and deal with poets of the next rank, we shall find that perfect truth and seriousness of matter, in close alliance with perfect truth and felicity of manner, is the rule no longer. We have now to take what we can get, to forego something here, to admit compensation for it there; to strike a balance, and to see how our poets stand in respect to one another when that balance has been struck. Let us observe how this is so.

We will take three poets, among the most considerable of our century : Leopardi, Byron, Wordsworth.   Giacomo Leopardi was ten years younger than Byron, and he died thirteen years after him ; both of them, therefore, died young—Byron at the age of thirty-six, Leopardi at the age of thirty-nine. Both of them were of noble birth, both of them suffered from physical defect, both of them were in revolt against the established facts and beliefs of their age ; but here the likeness between them ends.   The stricken poet of Recanati had no country, for an Italy in his day did not exist; he had no audience, no celebrity.   The volume of his poems, published in the very year of Byron's death, hardly sold, I suppose, its tens, while the volumes of Byron's poetry were selling their tens of thousands.   And yet Leopardi has the very qualities which we have found wanting to Byron ; he has the sense for form and style, the passion for just expression, the sure and firm touch of the

true artist. Nay, more, he has a grave fulness of
knowledge, an insight into the real bearings of the
questions which as a sceptical poet he raises, a
power of seizing the real point, a lucidity, with
which the author of *Cain* has nothing to compare.
I can hardly imagine Leopardi reading the

> '. . . And *thou* would'st go on aspiring
> To the great double Mysteries! the *two Principles!*'

or following Byron in his theological controversy
with Dr. Kennedy, without having his features
overspread by a calm and fine smile, and remark-
ing of his brilliant contemporary, as Goethe did,
that 'the moment he begins to reflect, he is a
child.' But indeed whoever wishes to feel the full
superiority of Leopardi over Byron in philosophic
thought, and in the expression of it, has only to
read one paragraph of one poem, the paragraph of
La Ginestra, beginning

> 'Sovente in queste piagge,'

and ending

> 'Non so se il riso o la pietà prevale.'

In like manner, Leopardi is at many points the poetic superior of Wordsworth too.   He has a far wider culture than Wordsworth, more mental lucidity, more freedom from illusions as to the real character of the established fact and of reigning conventions; above all, this Italian, with his pure and sure touch, with his fineness of perception, is far more of the artist.   Such a piece of pompous dulness as

'O for the coming of that glorious time,'

and all the rest of it, or such lumbering verse as Mr. Ruskin's enemy,

'Parching summer hath no warrant'—

would have been as impossible to Leopardi as to Dante.   Where, then, is Wordsworth's superiority? for the worth of what he has given us in poetry I hold to be greater, on the whole, than the worth of what Leopardi has given us.   It is in Wordsworth's sound and profound sense

'Of joy in widest commonalty spread;'

whereas Leopardi remains with his thoughts ever

fixed upon the *essenza insanabile*, upon the *acerbo, indegno mistero. delle cose.* It is in the power with which Wordsworth feels the resources of joy offered to us in nature, offered to us in the primary human affections and duties, and in the power with which, in his moments of inspiration, he renders this joy, and makes us, too, feel it; a force greater than himself seeming to lift him and to prompt his tongue, so that he speaks in a style far above any style of which he has the constant command, and with a truth far beyond any philosophic truth of which he has the conscious and assured possession. Neither Leopardi nor Wordsworth are of the same order with the great poets who made such verse as

Τλητὸν γὰρ Μοῖραι θυμὸν θέσαν ἀνθρώποισιν·

or as

'In la sua volontade e nostra pace ;

or as

'. . . Men must endure
Their going hence, even as their coming hither ;
Ripeness is all.'

But as compared with Leopardi, Wordsworth, though at many points less lucid, though far less a master of style, far less of an artist, gains so much by his criticism of life being, in certain matters of profound importance, healthful and true, whereas Leopardi's pessimism is not, that the value of Wordsworth's poetry, on the whole, stands higher for us than that of Leopardi's, as it stands higher for us, I think, than that of any modern poetry except Goethe's.

Byron's poetic value is also greater, on the whole, than Leopardi's; and his superiority turns in the same way upon the surpassing worth of something which he had and was, after all deduction has been made for his shortcomings. We. talk of Byron's *personality*, ' a personality in eminence such as has never been yet, and is not likely to come again ; ' and we say that by this personality Byron is ' different from all the rest of English poets, and in the main greater.' But can we not be a little more circumstantial, and name that in which the wonderful power of this personality consisted? We can; with the instinct of a poet Mr. Swinburne has seized upon it and named it for us. The power of Byron's personality lies in 'the splendid and imperishable excellence which covers all his offences and outweighs all his defects: *the excellence of sincerity and strength.*'

Byron found our nation, after its long and victorious struggle with revolutionary France, fixed in a system of established facts and dominant ideas which revolted him. The mental bondage of the most powerful part of our nation, of its strong middle-class, to a narrow and false system of this kind, is what we call British Philistinism. That bondage is unbroken to this hour, but in Byron's time it was even far more deep and dark than it is now. Byron was an aristocrat, and it is not difficult for an aristocrat to look on the prejudices and habits of the British Philistine with scepticism and disdain. Plenty of young men of his own class Byron met at Almack's or at Lady Jersey's, who regarded the established facts and reigning beliefs of the England of that day with as

o

little reverence as he did. But these men, disbelievers in British Philistinism in private, entered English public life, the most conventional in the world, and at once they saluted with respect the habits and ideas of British Philistinism as if they were a part of the order of creation, and as if in public no sane man would think of warring against them. With Byron it was different. What he called the *cant* of the great middle part of the English nation, what we call its Philistinism, revolted him; but the cant of his own class, deferring to this Philistinism and profiting by it, while they disbelieved in it, revolted him even more. ' Come what may,' are his own words, ' I will never flatter the million's canting in any shape.' His class in general, on the other hand, shrugged their shoulders at this cant, laughed at it, pandered to it, and ruled by it. The falsehood, cynicism, insolence, misgovernment, oppression, with their consequent unfailing crop of human misery, which were produced by this state of things, roused Byron to irreconcilable revolt and battle. They made him indignant, they infuriated him ; they were so strong, so defiant, so maleficent,—and yet he felt that they were doomed. 'You have seen every trampler down in turn,' he comforts himself with saying, 'from Buonaparte to the simplest individuals.' The old order, as after 1815 it stood victorious, with its ignorance and misery below, its cant, selfishness, and cynicism above, was at home and abroad equally hateful to him. 'I have simplified my politics,' he writes, 'into an utter detestation of all existing governments.' And again : 'Give me a republic. The king-times are fast finishing ; there will be blood shed like water and tears like mist, but the peoples will conquer in the end. I shall not live to see it, but I foresee it.'

Byron himself gave the preference, he tells us, to politicians and doers, far above writers and singers. But the politics of his own day and of his own class,—even of the Liberals of his own class,—were impossible for him. Nature had not formed him for a Liberal peer, proper to move the

Address in the House of Lords, to pay compliments
to the energy and self-reliance of British middle-
class Liberalism, and to adapt his politics to suit
it.   Unfitted for such politics, he threw himself
upon poetry as his organ ; and in poetry his topics
were not Queen Mab, and the Witch of Atlas, and
the Sensitive Plant—they were the upholders of
the old order, George the Third and Lord Castle-
reagh and the Duke of Wellington and Southey,
and they were the canters and tramplers of the
great world, and they were his enemies and himself.

Such was Byron's personality, by which ' he is
different from all the rest of English poets, and in
the main greater.'   But he posed all his life, says
M. Scherer.   Let us distinguish.   There is the
Byron who posed, there is the Byron with his
affectations and silliness, the Byron whose weakness Lady Blessington, with a woman's acuteness,
so admirably seized : ' His great defect is flippancy
and a total want of self-possession.'   But when
this theatrical and easily criticised personage be-

took himself to poetry, and when he had fairly warmed to his work, then he became another man ; then the theatrical personage passed away ; then a higher power took possession of him and filled him ; then at last came forth into light that true and puissant personality, with its direct strokes, its ever-welling force, its satire, its energy, and its agony. This is the real Byron ; whoever stops at the theatrical preludings does not know him. And this real Byron may well be superior to the stricken Leopardi, he may well be declared 'different from all the rest of English poets, and in the main greater,' in so far as it is true of him, as M. Taine well says, that 'all other souls, in comparison with his, seem inert' ; in so far as it is true of him that with superb, exhaustless energy, he maintained, as Professor Nichol well says, ' the struggle that keeps alive, if it does not save, the soul ;' in so far, finally, as he deserves (and he does deserve) the noble praise of him which I have already quoted from Mr. Swinburne ; the praise for ' the splendid and imperishable excellence which covers all his offences and outweighs all his defects : *the excellence of sincerity and strength.*'

True, as a man, Byron could not manage himself, could not guide his ways aright, but was all astray. True, he has no light, cannot lead us from the past to the future; 'the moment he reflects, he is a child.' The way out of the false state of things which enraged him he did not see, —the slow and laborious way upward; he had not the patience, knowledge, self-discipline, virtue, requisite for seeing it. True, also, as a poet, he has no fine and exact sense for word and structure and rhythm; he has not the artist's nature and gifts. Yet a personality of Byron's force counts for so much in life, and a rhetorician of Byron's force counts for so much in literature! But it would be most unjust to label Byron, as M. Scherer is disposed to label him, as a rhetorician only. Along with his astounding power and passion he had a strong and deep sense for what is beautiful in nature, and for what is beautiful in human action and suffering. When he warms to

his work, when he is inspired, Nature herself
seems to take the pen from him as she took it
from Wordsworth, and to write for him as she
wrote for Wordsworth, though in a different
fashion, with her own penetrating simplicity.
Goethe has well observed of Byron, that when he
is at his happiest his representation of things is
as easy and real as if he were improvising. It is
so ; and his verse then exhibits quite another and
a higher quality from the rhetorical quality,—
admirable as this also in its own kind of merit is,
—of such verse as

'Minions of splendour shrinking from distress,'

and of so much more verse of Byron's of that
stamp. Nature, I say, takes the pen for him ;
and then, assured master of a true poetic style
though he is not, any more than Wordsworth, yet
as from Wordsworth at his best there will come
such verse as

'Will no one tell me what she sings ?'

so from Byron, too, at his best, there will come

such verse as

> 'He heard it, but he heeded not; his eyes
> Were with his heart, and that was far away.'

Of verse of this high quality, Byron has much; of verse of a quality lower than this, of a quality rather rhetorical than truly poetic, yet still of extraordinary power and merit, he has still more. To separate, from the mass of poetry which Byron poured forth, all this higher portion, so superior to the mass, and still so considerable in quantity, and to present it in one body by itself, is to do a service, I believe, to Byron's reputation, and to the poetic glory of our country.

Such a service I have in the present volume attempted to perform. To Byron, after all the tributes which have been paid to him, here is yet one tribute more—

> 'Among thy mightier offerings here are mine!'

not a tribute of boundless homage certainly, but sincere; a tribute which consists not in covering the poet with eloquent eulogy of our own, but in letting him, at his best and greatest, speak for himself. Surely the critic who does most for his author is the critic who gains readers for his author himself, not for any lucubrations on his author ; — gains more readers for him, and enables those readers to read him with more admiration.

And in spite of his prodigious vogue, Byron has never yet, perhaps, had the serious admiration which he deserves. Society read him and talked about him, as it reads and talks about *Endymion* to-day ; and with the same sort of result. It looked in Byron's glass as it looks in Lord Beaconsfield's, and sees, or fancies that it sees, its own face there ; and then it goes its way, and straightway forgets what manner of man it saw. Even of his passionate admirers, how many never got beyond the theatrical Byron, from whom they caught the fashion of deranging their hair, or of knotting their neck-handkerchief, or of leaving their shirt-collar unbuttoned ; how few profoundly felt his vital influence, the influence of his splen-

did and imperishable excellence of sincerity and
strength!

His own aristocratic class, whose cynical make-
believe drove him to fury; the great middle-class,
on whose impregnable Philistinism he shattered
himself to pieces,—how little have either of these
felt Byron's vital influence! As the inevitable
break-up of the old order comes, as the English
middle-class slowly awakens from its intellectual
sleep of two centuries, as our actual present world,
to which this sleep has condemned us, shows itself
more clearly,—our world of an aristocracy materialised and null, a middle-class purblind and
hideous, a lower class crude and brutal,—we shall
turn our eyes again, and to more purpose, upon
this passionate and dauntless soldier of a forlorn
hope, who, ignorant of the future and unconsoled
by its promises, nevertheless waged against the
conservation of the old impossible world so fiery
battle; waged it till he fell,—waged it with such
splendid and imperishable excellence of sincerity
and strength.

Wordsworth's value is of another kind. Wordsworth has an insight into permanent sources of joy and consolation for mankind which Byron has not; his poetry gives us more which we may rest upon than Byron's,—more which we can rest upon now, and which men may rest upon always. I place Wordsworth's poetry, therefore, above Byron's on the whole, although in some points he was greatly Byron's inferior, and although Byron's poetry will always, probably, find more readers than Wordsworth's, and will give pleasure more easily. But these two, Wordsworth and Byron, stand, it seems to me, first and pre-eminent in actual performance, a glorious pair, among the English poets of this century. Keats had probably, indeed, a more consummate poetic gift than either of them; but he died having produced too little and being as yet too immature to rival them. I for my part can never even think of equalling with them any other of their contemporaries;—either Coleridge, poet and philosopher wrecked in a mist of opium; or Shelley, beautiful and ineffectual angel, beating in the void his luminous wings in vain. Wordsworth and Byron stand out by themselves. When the year 1900 is turned, and our nation comes to recount her poetic glories in the century which has then just ended, the first names with her will be these.

VII

SHELLEY [1]

NOWADAYS all things appear in print sooner or later; but I have heard from a lady who knew Mrs. Shelley a story of her which, so far as I know, has not appeared in print hitherto. Mrs. Shelley was choosing a school for her son, and asked the advice of this lady, who gave for advice —to use her own words to me—'Just the sort of banality, you know, one does come out with : Oh, send him somewhere where they will teach him to think for himself!' I have had far too long a training as a school inspector to presume to call an utterance of this kind a *banality*; however, it is not on this advice that I now wish to lay stress,

[1] Published in *The Nineteenth Century*, January 1888.

but upon Mrs. Shelley's reply to it. Mrs. Shelley answered: 'Teach him to think for himself? Oh, my God, teach him rather to think like other people!'

To the lips of many and many a reader of Professor Dowden's volumes a cry of this sort will surely rise, called forth by Shelley's life as there delineated. I have read those volumes with the deepest interest, but I regret their publication, and am surprised, I confess, that Shelley's family should have desired or assisted it. For my own part, at any rate, I would gladly have been left with the impression, the ineffaceable impression, made upon me by Mrs. Shelley's first edition of her husband's collected poems. Medwin and Hogg and Trelawny had done little to change the impression made by those four delightful volumes of the original edition of 1839. The text of the poems has in some places been mended since; but Shelley is not a classic, whose various readings are to be noted with earnest attention. The charm of the poems flowed in upon us from that edition

and the charm of the character.   Mrs. Shelley had
done her work admirably; her introductions to
the poems of each year, with Shelley's prefaces
and passages from his letters, supplied the very
picture of Shelley to be desired.   Somewhat
idealised by tender regret and exalted memory
Mrs. Shelley's representation no doubt was.   But
without sharing her conviction that Shelley's character, impartially judged, 'would stand in fairer
and brighter light than that of any contemporary,'
we learned from her to know the soul of affection,
of 'gentle and cordial goodness,' of eagerness and
ardour for human happiness, which was in this
rare spirit—so mere a monster unto many.   Mrs.
Shelley said in her general preface to her husband's poems : 'I abstain from any remark on the
occurrences of his private life, except inasmuch as
the passions which they engendered inspired his
poetry; this is not the time to relate the truth.'   I
for my part could wish, I repeat, that that time
had never come.

But come it has, and Professor Dowden has given

us the Life of Percy Bysshe Shelley in two very thick volumes. If the work was to be done, Professor Dowden has indeed done it thoroughly. One or two things in his biography of Shelley I could wish different, even waiving the question whether it was desirable to relate in full the occurrences of Shelley's private life. Professor Dowden holds a brief for Shelley ; he pleads for Shelley as an advocate pleads for his client, and this strain of pleading, united with an attitude of adoration which in Mrs. Shelley had its charm, but which Professor Dowden was not bound to adopt from her, is unserviceable to Shelley, nay, injurious to him, because it inevitably begets, in many readers of the story which Professor Dowden has to tell, impatience and revolt. Further, let me remark that the biography before us is of prodigious length, although its hero died before he was thirty years old, and that it might have been considerably shortened if it had been more plainly and simply written. I see that one of Professor Dowden's critics, while praising his style for ' a certain poetic

quality of fervour and picturesqueness,' laments
that in some important passages Professor Dowden 'fritters away great opportunities for sustained
and impassioned narrative.' I am inclined much
rather to lament that Professor Dowden has not
steadily kept his poetic quality of fervour and
picturesqueness more under control. Is it that
the Home Rulers have so loaded the language that
even an Irishman who is not one of them catches
something of their full habit of style? No, it is
rather, I believe, that Professor Dowden, of poetic
nature himself, and dealing with a poetic nature
like Shelley, is so steeped in sentiment by his
subject that in almost every page of the biography
the sentiment runs over. A curious note of his
style, suffused with sentiment, is that it seems
incapable of using the common word *child*. A
great many births are mentioned in the biography,
but always it is a poetic *babe* that is born, not
a prosaic *child*. And so, again, André Chénier
is not guillotined, but 'too foully done to death.'
Again, Shelley after his runaway marriage with

P

Harriet Westbrook was in Edinburgh without money and full of anxieties for the future, and complained of his hard lot in being unable to get away, in being 'chained to the filth and commerce of Edinburgh.' Natural enough; but why should Professor Dowden improve the occasion as follows? 'The most romantic of northern cities could lay no spell upon his spirit. His eye was not fascinated by the presences of mountains and the sea, by the fantastic outlines of aërial piles seen amid the wreathing smoke of Auld Reekie, by the gloom of the Canongate illuminated with shafts of sunlight streaming from its interesting wynds and alleys; nor was his imagination kindled by storied house or palace, and the voices of old, forgotten, far-off things, which haunt their walls.' If Professor Dowden, writing a book in prose, could have brought himself to eschew poetic excursions of this kind and to tell his story in a plain way, lovers of simplicity of whom there are some still left in the world, would have been gratified, and at the same time his book would have been the shorter by scores of pages.

These reserves being made, I have little except praise for the manner in which Professor Dowden has performed his task; whether it was a task which ought to be performed at all, probably did not lie with him to decide. His ample materials are used with order and judgment; the history of Shelley's life develops itself clearly before our eyes; the documents of importance for it are given with sufficient fulness, nothing essential seems to have been kept back, although I would gladly, I confess, have seen more of Miss Clairmont's journal, whatever arrangement she may in her later life have chosen to exercise upon it. In general all documents are so fairly and fully cited, that Professor Dowden's pleadings for Shelley, though they may sometimes indispose and irritate the reader, produce no obscuring of the truth; the documents manifest it of themselves. Last but not least of Professor Dowden's merits, he has provided his book with an excellent index.

Undoubtedly this biography, with its full

account of the occurrences of Shelley's private
life, compels one to review one's former impression of him. Undoubtedly the brilliant and
attaching rebel who in thinking for himself had
of old our sympathy so passionately with him,
when we come to read his full biography makes
us often and often inclined to cry out: 'My God!
he had far better have thought like other people.'
There is a passage in Hogg's capitally written and
most interesting account of Shelley which I wrote
down when I first read it and have borne in mind
ever since; so beautifully it seemed to render the
true Shelley. Hogg has been speaking of the intellectual expression of Shelley's features, and he
goes on: 'Nor was the moral expression less
beautiful than the intellectual; for there was a
softness, a delicacy, a gentleness, and especially
(though this will surprise many) that air of profound religious veneration that characterises the
best works and chiefly the frescoes (and into these
they infused their whole souls) of the great masters
of Florence and of Rome.' What we have of

Shelley in poetry and prose suited with this charming picture of him; Mrs. Shelley's account suited with it; it was a possession which one would gladly have kept unimpaired. It still subsists, I must now add; it subsists even after one has read the present biography; it subsists, but so as by fire. It subsists with many a scar and stain; never again will it have the same pureness and beauty which it had formerly. I regret this, as I have said, and I confess I do not see what has been gained. Our ideal Shelley was the true Shelley after all; what has been gained by making us at moments doubt it? What has been gained by forcing upon us much in him which is ridiculous and odious, by compelling any fair mind, if it is to retain with a good conscience its ideal Shelley, to do that which I propose to do now? I propose to mark firmly what is ridiculous and odious in the Shelley brought to our knowledge by the new materials, and then to show that our former beautiful and lovable Shelley nevertheless survives.

Almost everybody knows the main outline of the events of Shelley's life. It will be necessary for me, however, up to the date of his second marriage, to go through them here. Percy Bysshe Shelley was born at Field Place, near Horsham, in Sussex, on the 4th of August 1792. He was of an old family of country gentlemen, and the heir to a baronetcy. He had one brother and five sisters, but the brother so much younger than himself as to be no companion for him in his boyhood at home, and after he was separated from home and England he never saw him. Shelley was brought up at Field Place with his sisters. At ten years old he was sent to a private school at Isleworth, where he read Mrs. Radcliffe's romances and was fascinated by a popular scientific lecturer. After two years of private school he went in 1804 to Eton. Here he took no part in cricket or football, refused to fag, was known as 'mad Shelley' and much tormented; when tormented beyond endurance he could be dangerous. Certainly he was not happy at Eton; but he had friends, he boated, he rambled about the country. His school lessons were easy to him, and his reading extended far beyond them; he read books on chemistry, he read Pliny's *Natural History*, Godwin's *Political Justice*, Lucretius, Franklin, Condorcet. It is said he was called 'atheist Shelley' at Eton, but this is not so well established as his having been called 'mad Shelley.' He was full, at any rate, of new and revolutionary ideas, and he declared at a later time that he was twice expelled from the school but recalled through the interference of his father.

In the spring of 1810 Shelley, now in his eighteenth year, entered University College, Oxford, as an exhibitioner. He had already written novels and poems; a poem on the Wandering Jew, in seven or eight cantos, he sent to Campbell, and was told by Campbell that there were but two good lines in it. He had solicited the correspondence of Mrs. Hemans, then Felicia Browne and unmarried; he had fallen in love with a charming cousin, Harriet Grove. In the autumn of 1810 he

found a publisher for his verse; he also found a
friend in a very clever and free-minded commoner
of his college, Thomas Jefferson Hogg, who has
admirably described the Shelley of those Oxford
days, with his chemistry, his eccentric habits, his
charm of look and character, his conversation, his
shrill discordant voice. Shelley read incessantly.
Hume's *Essays* produced a powerful impression on
him; his free speculation led him to what his
father, and worse still his cousin Harriet, thought
'detestable principles'; his cousin and his family
became estranged from him. He, on his part,
became more and more incensed against the
'bigotry' and 'intolerance' which produced such
estrangement. 'Here I swear, and as I break my
oaths, may Infinity, Eternity, blast me—here I
swear that never will I forgive intolerance.' At
the beginning of 1811 he prepared and published
what he called a 'leaflet for letters,' having for its
title *The Necessity of Atheism*. He sent copies to
all the bishops, to the Vice-Chancellor of Oxford,
and to the heads of houses. On Lady Day he was

summoned before the authorities of his College, refused to answer the question whether he had written *The Necessity of Atheism*, told the Master and Fellows that 'their proceedings would become a court of inquisitors but not free men in a free country,' and was expelled for contumacy. Hogg wrote a letter of remonstrance to the authorities, was in his turn summoned before them and questioned as to his share in the 'leaflet,' and, refusing to answer, he also was expelled.

Shelley settled with Hogg in lodgings in London. His father, excusably indignant, was not a wise man and managed his son ill. His plan of recommending Shelley to read Paley's *Natural Theology*, and of *reading it with him himself*, makes us smile. Shelley, who about this time wrote of his younger sister, then at school at Clapham, 'There are some hopes of this dear little girl, she would be a divine little scion of infidelity if I could get hold of her,' was not to have been cured by Paley's *Natural Theology* administered through Mr. Timothy Shelley. But by the middle of May

Shelley's father had agreed to allow him two
hundred pounds a year.   Meanwhile in visiting his
sisters at their school in Clapham, Shelley made
the acquaintance of a schoolfellow of theirs, Harriet
Westbrook.   She was a beautiful and lively girl,
with a father who had kept a tavern in Mount
Street, but had now retired from business, and one
sister much older than herself, who encouraged in
every possible way the acquaintance of her sister
of sixteen with the heir to a baronetcy and a great
estate.   Soon Shelley heard that Harriet met with
cold looks at her school for associating with an
atheist; his generosity and his ready indignation
against 'intolerance' were roused.   In the summer
Harriet wrote to him that she was persecuted not
at school only but at home also, that she was lonely
and miserable, and would gladly put an end to her
life.   Shelley went to see her; she owned her love
for him, and he engaged himself to her.   He told
his cousin Charles Grove that his happiness had
been blighted when the other Harriet, Charles's
sister, cast him off; that now the only thing worth

living for was self-sacrifice. Harriet's persecutors became yet more troublesome, and Shelley, at the end of August, went off with her to Edinburgh and they were married. The entry in the register is this :—

'*August* 28, 1811.—Percy Bysshe Shelley, farmer, Sussex, and Miss Harriet Westbrook, St. Andrew Church Parish, daughter of Mr. John Westbrook, London.'

After five weeks in Edinburgh the young farmer and his wife came southwards and took lodgings at York, under the shadow of what Shelley calls that 'gigantic pile of superstition,' the Minster. But his friend Hogg was in a lawyer's office in York, and Hogg's society made the Minster endurable. Mr. Timothy Shelley's happiness in his son was naturally not increased by the runaway marriage ; he stopped his allowance, and Shelley determined to visit ' this thoughtless man,' as he calls his parent, and to ' try the force of truth' upon him. Nothing could be effected : Shelley's mother, too, was now against him. He returned to York to find that in his absence his friend Hogg had been making love to Harriet, who had indignantly repulsed him. Shelley was shocked, but after a 'terrible day' of explanation from Hogg, he 'fully, freely pardoned him,' promised to retain him still as 'his friend, his bosom friend,' and 'hoped soon to convince him how lovely virtue was.' But for the present it seemed better to separate. In November he and Harriet, with her sister Eliza, took a cottage at Keswick. Shelley was now in great straits for money; the great Sussex neighbour of the Shelley's, the Duke of Norfolk, interposed in his favour, and his father and grandfather seem to have offered him at this time an income of £2000 a year, if he would consent to entail the family estate. Shelley indignantly refused to 'forswear his principles,' by accepting 'a proposal so insultingly hateful.' But in December his father agreed, though with an ill grace, to grant him his allowance of £200 a year again, and Mr. Westbrook promised to allow a like sum to his daughter. So after four months of marriage the

Shelleys began 1812 with an income of £400 a year.

Early in February they left Keswick and proceeded to Dublin, where Shelley, who had prepared an address to the Catholics, meant to 'devote himself towards forwarding the great ends of virtue and happiness in Ireland.' Before leaving Keswick he wrote to William Godwin, 'the regulator and former of his mind,' making profession of his mental obligations to him, of his respect and veneration, and soliciting Godwin's friendship. A correspondence followed ; Godwin pronounced his young disciple's plans for 'disseminating the doctrines of philanthropy and freedom' in Ireland to be unwise; Shelley bowed to his mentor's decision and gave up his Irish campaign, quitting Dublin on the 4th of April 1812. He and Harriet wandered first to Nant-Gwillt in South Wales, near the upper Wye, and from thence after a month or two to Lynmouth in North Devon, where he busied himself with his poem of *Queen Mab*, and with sending to sea boxes and bottles

containing a *Declaration of Rights* by him, in the
hope that the winds and waves might carry his
doctrines where they would do good.   But his
Irish servant, bearing the prophetic name of Healy,
posted the *Declaration* on the walls of Barnstaple
and was taken up ; Shelley found himself watched
and no longer able to enjoy Lynmouth in peace.
He moved in September 1812 to Tremadoc, in
North Wales, where he threw himself ardently
into an enterprise for recovering a great stretch of
drowned land from the sea.   But at the beginning
of October he and Harriet visited London, and
Shelley grasped Godwin by the hand at last.   At
once an intimacy arose, but the future Mary
Shelley — Godwin's daughter by his first wife,
Mary Wollstonecraft—was absent on a visit in
Scotland when the Shelleys arrived in London.
They became acquainted, however, with the second
Mrs. Godwin, on whom we have Charles Lamb's
friendly comment : ' A very disgusting woman, and
wears green spectacles ! ' with the amiable Fanny,
Mary Wollstonecraft's daughter by Imlay, before

her marriage with Godwin ; and probably also
with Jane Clairmont, the second Mrs. Godwin's
daughter by a first marriage, and herself, afterwards the mother of Byron's Allegra. Complicated
relationships, as in the Theban story ! and there
will be not wanting, presently, something of the
Theban horrors. During this visit of six weeks to
London Shelley renewed his intimacy with Hogg ;
in the middle of November he returned to Tremadoc. There he remained until the end of February
1813, perfectly happy with Harriet, reading widely,
and working at his *Queen Mab* and at the notes to
that poem. On the 26th of February an attempt
was made, or so he fancied, to assassinate him,
and in high nervous excitement he hurriedly left
Tremadoc and repaired with Harriet to Dublin
again. On this visit to Ireland he saw Killarney,
but early in April he and Harriet were back again
in London.

There in June 1813 their daughter Ianthe was
born ; at the end of July they moved to Bracknell,
in Berkshire. They had for neighbours there a

Mrs. Boinville and her married daughter, whom Shelley found to be fascinating women, with a culture which to his wife was altogether wanting. Cornelia Turner, Mrs. Boinville's daughter, was melancholy, required consolation, and found it, Hogg tells us, in Petrarch's poetry; 'Bysshe entered at once fully into her views and caught the soft infection, breathing the tenderest and sweetest melancholy as every true poet ought.' Peacock, a man of keen and cultivated mind, joined the circle at Bracknell. He and Harriet, not yet eighteen, used sometimes to laugh at the gushing sentiment and enthusiasm of the Bracknell circle; Harriet had also given offence to Shelley by getting a wet-nurse for her child; in Professor Dowden's words, 'the beauty of Harriet's motherly relation to her babe was marred in Shelley's eyes by the introduction into his home of a hireling nurse to whom was delegated the mother's tenderest office.' But in September Shelley wrote a sonnet to his child which expresses his deep love for the mother also, to whom in

March 1814 he was remarried in London, lest the Scotch marriage should prove to have been in any point irregular. Harriet's sister Eliza, however, whom Shelley had at first treated with excessive deference, had now become hateful to him. And in the very month of the London marriage we find him writing to Hogg that he is staying with the Boinvilles, having 'escaped, in the society of all that philosophy and friendship combine, from the dismaying solitude of myself.' Cornelia Turner, he adds, whom he once thought cold and reserved 'is the reverse of this, as she is the reverse of everything bad; she inherits all the divinity of her mother. Then comes a stanza, beginning

> 'Thy dewy looks sink in my breast,
> Thy gentle words stir poison there.'

It has no meaning, he says; it is only written in thought. 'It is evident from this pathetic letter,' says Professor Dowden, 'that Shelley's happiness in his home had been fatally stricken.' This is a curious way of putting the matter. To me what is evident is rather that Shelley had, to use Professor Dowden's words again—for in these things of high sentiment I gladly let him speak for me—' a too vivid sense that here (in the society of the Boinville family) were peace and joy and gentleness and love.' In April come some more verses to the Boinvilles, which contain the first good stanza that Shelley wrote. In May comes a poem to Harriet, of which Professor Dowden's prose analysis is as poetic as the poem itself. 'If she has something to endure (from the Boinville attachment), it is not much, and all her husband's weal hangs upon her loving endurance, for see how pale and wildered anguish has made him!' Harriet, unconvinced, seems to have gone off to Bath in resentment, from whence, however, she kept up a constant correspondence with Shelley, who was now of age, and busy in London raising money on post-obit bonds for his own wants and those of the friend and former of his mind, Godwin.

And now, indeed, it was to become true that if from the inflammable Shelley's devotion to the

Boinville family poor Harriet had had 'something to endure,' yet this was 'not much' compared with what was to follow. At Godwin's house Shelley met Mary Wollstonecraft Godwin, his future wife, then in her seventeenth year. She was a gifted person, but, as Professor Dowden says, she 'had breathed during her entire life an atmosphere of free thought.' On the 8th of June Hogg called at Godwin's with Shelley; Godwin was out, but 'a door was partially and softly opened, a thrilling voice called "Shelley!" a thrilling voice answered "Mary!"' Shelley's summoner was 'a very young female, fair and fair-haired, pale indeed, and with a piercing look, wearing a frock of tartan.' Already they were 'Shelley' and 'Mary' to one another; 'before the close of June they knew and felt,' says Professor Dowden, 'that each was to the other inexpressibly dear.' The churchyard of St. Pancras where her mother was buried, became 'a place now doubly sacred to Mary, since on one eventful day Bysshe here poured forth his griefs, his hopes, his love, and she, in sign of everlasting union, placed her hand in his.' In July Shelley gave her a copy of *Queen Mab*, printed but not published, and under the tender dedication to Harriet he wrote : 'Count Slobendorf was about to marry a woman who, attracted solely by his fortune, proved her selfishness by deserting him in prison.' Mary added an inscription on her part : 'I love the author beyond all powers of expression . . . by that love we have promised to each other, although I may not be yours I can never be another's,'—and a good deal more to the same effect.

Amid these excitements Shelley was for some days without writing to Harriet, who applied to Hookham the publisher to know what had happened. She was expecting her confinement ; 'I always fancy something dreadful has happened,' she wrote, 'if I do not hear from him . . . I cannot endure this dreadful state of suspense.' Shelley then wrote to her, begging her to come to London ; and when she arrived there, he told her the state of his feelings, and proposed separation. The shock made Harriet ill ; and Shelley, says Peacock, 'between his old feelings towards Harriet, and his new passion for Mary, showed in his looks, in his gestures, in his speech, the state of a mind "suffering, like a little kingdom, the nature of an insurrection."' Godwin grew uneasy about his daughter, and after a serious talk with her, wrote to Shelley. Under such circumstances, Professor Dowden tells us, 'to youth, swift and decisive measures seem the best.' In the early morning of the 28th of July 1814 'Mary Godwin stepped across her father's threshold into the summer air,' she and Shelley went off together in a post-chaise to Dover, and from thence crossed to the Continent.

On the 14th of August the fugitives were at Troyes on their way to Switzerland. From Troyes Shelley addressed a letter to Harriet, of which the best description I can give is that it is precisely the letter which a man in the writer's circumstances should not have written.

'My dearest Harriet (he begins).—I write to you from this detestable town; I write to show that

I do not forget you; I write to urge you to come to Switzerland, where you will at last find one firm and constant friend to whom your interests will be always dear—by whom your feelings will never wilfully be injured. From none can you expect this but me—all else are either unfeeling or selfish, or have be-loved friends of their own.'

Then follows a description of his journey with Mary from Paris, 'through a fertile country, neither interesting from the character of its in-habitants nor the beauty of the scenery, with a mule to carry our baggage, as Mary, who has not been sufficiently well to walk, fears the fatigue of walking.' Like St. Paul to Timothy, he ends with commissions :—

'I wish you to bring with you the two deeds which Tahourdin has to prepare for you, as also a copy of the settlement. Do not part with any of your money. But what shall be done about the books? You can consult on the spot. With love to my sweet little Ianthe, ever most affectionately yours, S.

'I write in great haste; we depart directly.'

Professor Dowden's flow of sentiment is here so agitating, that I relieve myself by resorting to a drier world. Certainly my comment on this letter shall not be his, that it 'assures Harriet that her interests were still dear to Shelley, though now their lives had moved apart.' But neither will I call the letter an odious letter, a hideous letter. I prefer to call it, applying an untranslatable French word, a *bête* letter. And it is *bête* from what is the signal, the disastrous want and weakness of Shelley, with all his fine intellectual gifts—his utter deficiency in humour.

Harriet did not accept Shelley's invitation to join him and Mary in Switzerland. Money difficulties drove the travellers back to England in September. Godwin would not see Shelley, but he sorely needed, continually demanded and eagerly accepted, pecuniary help from his erring 'spiritual son.' Between Godwin's wants and his own, Shelley was hard pressed. He got from Harriet, who still believed that he would return to her, twenty pounds which remained in her hands. In November she was confined ; a son and heir was born to Shelley. He went to see Harriet, but 'the interview left husband and wife each embittered against the other.' Friends were severe; 'when Mrs. Boinville wrote, her letter seemed cold and even sarcastic,' says Professor Dowden. 'Solitude,' he continues, 'unharassed by debts and duns, with Mary's companionship, the society of a few friends, and the delights of study and authorship, would have made these winter months to Shelley months of unusual happiness and calm.' But, alas! creditors were pestering, and even Harriet gave trouble. In January 1815 Mary had to write in her journal this entry: 'Harriet sends her creditors here; nasty woman. Now we must change our lodgings.'

One day about this time Shelley asked Peacock, 'Do you think Wordsworth could have written such poetry if he ever had dealings with money-lenders?' Not only had Shelley dealings with money-lenders, he now had dealings with bailiffs also. But still he continued to read largely. In January 1815 his grandfather, Sir Bysshe Shelley, died. Shelley went down into Sussex; his father would not suffer him to enter the house.

but he sat outside the door and read *Comus*, while
the reading of his grandfather's will went on in-
side.   In February was born Mary's first child, a
girl, who lived but a few days.   All the spring
Shelley was ill and harassed, but by June it was
settled that he should have an allowance from his
father of £1000 a year, and that his debts (includ-
ing £1200 promised by him to Godwin) should be
paid.   He on his part paid Harriet's debts and
allowed her £200 a year.   In August he took a
house on the borders of Windsor Park, and made
a boating excursion up the Thames as far as Lechlade, an excursion which produced his first entire
poem of value, the beautiful *Stanzas in Lechlade
Churchyard*.   They were followed, later in the
autumn, by *Alastor*.   Henceforth, from this winter
of 1815 until he was drowned between Leghorn and
Spezzia in July 1822, Shelley's literary history is
sufficiently given in the delightful introductions
prefixed by Mrs. Shelley to the poems of each year.
Much of the history of his life is there given also ;
but with some of those 'occurrences of his private

life' on which Mrs. Shelley forbore to touch, and
which are now made known to us in Professor
Dowden's book, we have still to deal.

Mary's first son, William, was born in January
1816, and in February we find Shelley declaring
himself 'strongly urged, by the perpetual experience of neglect or enmity from almost every one
but those who are supported by my resources, to
desert my native country, hiding myself and Mary
from the contempt which we so unjustly endure.'
Early in May he left England with Mary and
Miss Clairmont; they met Lord Byron at Geneva
and passed the summer by the Lake of Geneva
in his company. Miss Clairmont had already in
London, without the knowledge of the Shelleys,
made Byron's acquaintance and become his mistress. Shelley determined, in the course of the
summer, to go back to England, and, after all, 'to
make that most excellent of nations my perpetual
resting-place.' In September he and his ladies
returned; Miss Clairmont was then expecting her
confinement. Of her being Byron's mistress the

Shelleys were now aware ; but 'the moral indignation,' says Professor Dowden, 'which Byron's
act might justly arouse, seems to have been felt by
neither Shelley nor Mary.' If Byron and Claire
Clairmont, as she was now called, loved and were
happy, all was well.

The eldest daughter of the Godwin household,
the amiable Fanny, was unhappy at home and in
deep dejection of spirits. Godwin was, as usual,
in terrible straits for money. The Shelleys and
Miss Clairmont settled themselves at Bath ; early
in October Fanny Godwin passed through Bath
without their knowing it, travelled on to Swansea,
took a bedroom at the hotel there, and was found
in the morning dead, with a bottle of laudanum on
the table beside her and these words in her hand-
writing :—

'I have long determined that the best thing I
could do was to put an end to the existence of a
being whose birth was unfortunate,[1] and whose life

---

[1] She was Mary Wollstonecraft's natural daughter by
Imlay.

has only been a series of pain to those persons who have hurt their health in endeavouring to promote her welfare.   Perhaps to hear of my death will give you pain, but you will soon have the blessing of forgetting that such a creature ever existed as . . .'

There is no signature.

A sterner tragedy followed.   On the 9th of November 1816 Harriet Shelley left the house in Brompton where she was then living, and did not return.   On the 10th of December her body was found in the Serpentine; she had drowned herself. In one respect Professor Dowden resembles Providence : his ways are inscrutable.   His comment on Harriet's death is : 'There is no doubt she wandered from the ways of upright living.'   But, he adds : 'That no act of Shelley's, during the two years which immediately preceded her death, tended to cause the rash act which brought her life to its close, seems certain.'   Shelley had been living with Mary all the time; only that!

On the 30th of December 1816 Mary Godwin and Shelley were married.   I shall pursue 'the occurrences of Shelley's private life' no further

For the five years and a half which remain, Professor Dowden's book adds to our knowledge of Shelley's life much that is interesting; but what was chiefly important we knew already. The new and grave matter which we did not know, or knew in the vaguest way only, but which Shelley's family and Professor Dowden have now thought it well to give us in full, ends with Shelley's second marriage.

I regret, I say once more, that it has been given. It is a sore trial for our love of Shelley. What a set! what a world! is the exclamation that breaks from us as we come to an end of this history of 'the occurrences of Shelley's private life.' I used the French word *bête* for a letter of Shelley's; for the world in which we find him I can only use another French word, *sale*. Godwin's house of sordid horror, and Godwin preaching and holding the hat, and the green - spectacled Mrs. Godwin, and Hogg the faithful friend, and Hunt the Horace of this precious world, and, to go up higher, Sir Timothy Shelley, a great country gentle-

man, feeling himself safe while 'the exalted mind
of the Duke of Norfolk [the drinking Duke] protects me with the world,' and Lord Byron with his
deep grain of coarseness and commonness, his
affectation, his brutal selfishness — what a set!
The history carries us to Oxford, and I think of
the clerical and respectable Oxford of those old
times, the Oxford of Copleston and the Kebles
and Hawkins, and a hundred more, with the relief
Keble declares himself to experience from Izaak
Walton,

'When, wearied with the tale thy times disclose,
    The eye first finds thee out in thy secure repose.'

I am not only thinking of morals and the house of
Godwin, I am thinking also of tone, bearing,
dignity. I appeal to Cardinal Newman, if per-
chance he does me the honour to read these words,
is it possible to imagine Copleston or Hawkins
declaring himself safe 'while the exalted mind
of the Duke of Norfolk protects me with the
world'?

Mrs. Shelley, after her marriage and during Shelley's closing years, becomes attractive; up to her marriage her letters and journal do not please. Her ability is manifest, but she is not attractive. In the world discovered to us by Professor Dowden as surrounding Shelley up to 1817, the most pleasing figure is poor Fanny Godwin; after Fanny Godwin, the most pleasing figure is Harriet Shelley herself.

Professor Dowden's treatment of Harriet is not worthy—so much he must allow me in all kindness, but also in all seriousness, to say—of either his taste or his judgment. His pleading for Shelley is constant, and he does more harm than good to Shelley by it. But here his championship of Shelley makes him very unjust to a cruelly used and unhappy girl. For several pages he balances the question whether or not Harriet was unfaithful to Shelley before he left her for Mary, and he leaves the question unsettled. As usual Professor Dowden (and it is his signal merit) supplies the evidence decisive against himself

Thornton Hunt, not well disposed to Harriet, Hogg, Peacock, Trelawny, Hookham, and a member of Godwin's own family, are all clear in their evidence that up to her parting from Shelley Harriet was perfectly innocent. But that precious witness, Godwin, wrote in 1817 that 'she had proved herself unfaithful to her husband before their separation. . . . Peace be to her shade!' Why, Godwin was the father of Harriet's successor. But Mary believed the same thing. She was Harriet's successor. But Shelley believed it too. He had it from Godwin. But he was convinced of it earlier. The evidence for this is, that, in writing to Southey in 1820, Shelley declares that 'the single passage of a life, otherwise not only spotless but spent in an impassioned pursuit of virtue, which looks like a blot,' bears that appearance 'merely because I regulated my domestic arrangements without deferring to the notions of the vulgar, although I might have done so quite as conveniently had I descended to their base thoughts.' From this Professor Dowden con-

cludes that Shelley believed he could have got a
divorce from Harriet had he so wished. The
conclusion is not clear. But even were the
evidence perfectly clear that Shelley believed
Harriet unfaithful when he parted from her, we
should have to take into account Mrs. Shelley's
most true sentence in her introduction to *Alastor* :
'In all Shelley did, he, at the time of doing it,
believed himself justified to his own conscience.'

Shelley's asserting a thing vehemently does not
prove more than that he chose to believe it and
did believe it. His extreme and violent changes
of opinion about people show this sufficiently.
Eliza Westbrook is at one time 'a diamond not
so large' as her sister Harriet but 'more highly
polished'; and then : 'I certainly hate her with
all my heart and soul. I sometimes feel faint
with the fatigue of checking the overflowings of
my unbounded abhorrence for this miserable
wretch.' The antipathy, Hogg tells us, was as
unreasonable as the former excess of deference.
To his friend Miss Hitchener he says : 'Never

R

shall that intercourse cease, which has been the
day-dawn of my existence, the sun which has
shed warmth on the cold drear length of the
anticipated prospect of life.' A little later, and
she has become 'the Brown Demon, a woman of
desperate views and dreadful passions, but of cool
and undeviating revenge.' Even Professor Dowden admits that this is absurd; that the real Miss
Hitchener was not seen by Shelley, either when
he adored or when he detested.

Shelley's power of persuading himself was equal
to any occasion; but would not his conscientiousness and high feeling have prevented his exerting
this power at poor Harriet's expense? To abandon
her as he did, must he not have known her
to be false? Professor Dowden insists always
on Shelley's 'conscientiousness.' Shelley himself
speaks of his 'impassioned pursuit of virtue.'
Leigh Hunt compared his life to that of 'Plato
himself, or, still more, a Pythagorean,' and added
that he 'never met a being who came nearer,
perhaps so near, to the height of humanity,' to

being an 'angel of charity.' In many respects
Shelley really resembled both a Pythagorean and
an angel of charity. He loved high thoughts, he
cared nothing for sumptuous lodging, fare, and
raiment, he was poignantly afflicted at the sight
of misery, he would have given away his last
farthing, would have suffered in his own person,
to relieve it. But in one important point he was
like neither a Pythagorean nor an angel : he was
extremely inflammable. Professor Dowden leaves
no doubt on the matter. After reading his book,
one feels sickened for ever of the subject of
irregular relations; God forbid that I should
go into the scandals about Shelley's ' Neapolitan
charge,' about Shelley and Emilia Viviani, about
Shelley and Miss Clairmont, and the rest of it !
I will say only that it is visible enough that when
the passion of love was aroused in Shelley (and it
was aroused easily) one could not be sure of him,
his friends could not trust him. We have seen
him with the Boinville family. With Emilia
Viviani he is the same. If he is left much alone

with Miss Clairmont, he evidently makes Mary uneasy ; nay, he makes Professor Dowden himself uneasy. And I conclude that an entirely human inflammability, joined to an inhuman want of humour and a superhuman power of self-deception, are the causes which chiefly explain Shelley's abandonment of Harriet in the first place, and then his behaviour to her and his defence of himself afterwards.

His misconduct to Harriet, his want of humour, his self-deception, are fully brought before us for the first time by Professor Dowden's book. Good morals and good criticism alike forbid that when all this is laid bare to us we should deny, or hide, or extenuate it. Nevertheless I go back after all to what I said at the beginning; still our ideal Shelley, the angelic Shelley, subsists. Unhappily the data for this Shelley we had and knew long ago, while the data for the unattractive Shelley are fresh ; and what is fresh is likely to fix our attention more than what is familiar. But Professor Dowden's volumes, which give so much, which give

too much, also afford data for picturing anew the
Shelley who delights, as well as for picturing for
the first time a Shelley who, to speak plainly,
disgusts ; and with what may renew and restore
our impression of the delightful Shelley I shall
end.

The winter at Marlow, and the ophthalmia
caught among the cottages of the poor, we knew,
but we have from Professor Dowden more details of
this winter and of Shelley's work among the poor ;
we have above all, for the first time I believe, a
line of verse of Shelley's own which sums up truly
and perfectly this most attractive side of him—

'I am the friend of the unfriended poor.'

But that in Shelley on which I would especially
dwell is that in him which contrasts most with
the ignobleness of the world in which we have
seen him living, and with the pernicious nonsense
which we have found him talking. The Shelley
of 'marvellous gentleness,' of feminine refinement,
with gracious and considerate manners, 'a perfect

gentleman, entirely without arrogance or aggressive egotism,' completely devoid of the proverbial and ferocious vanity of authors and poets, always disposed to make little of his own work and to prefer that of others, of reverent enthusiasm for the great and wise, of high and tender seriousness, of heroic generosity, and of a delicacy in rendering services which was equal to his generosity—the Shelley who was all this is the Shelley with whom I wish to end. He may talk nonsense about tyrants and priests, but what a high and noble ring in such a sentence as the following, written by a young man who is refusing £2000 a year rather than consent to entail a great property!

'That I should entail £120,000 of command over labour, of power to remit this, to employ it for benevolent purposes, on one whom I know not—who might, instead of being the benefactor of mankind, be its bane, or use this for the worst purposes, which the real delegates of my chance - given property might convert into a most useful instrument of benevolence! No! this you will not suspect me of.'

And again :—

'I desire money because I think I know the use
of it. It commands labour, it gives leisure ; and to
give leisure to those who will employ it in the forwarding of truth is the noblest present an individual
can make to the whole.'

If there is extravagance here, it is extravagance
of a beautiful and rare sort, like Shelley's ' underhand ways ' also, which differed singularly, the
cynic Hogg tells us, from the underhand ways of
other people ; ' the latter were concealed because
they were mean, selfish, sordid ; Shelley's secrets,
on the contrary (kindnesses done by stealth), were
hidden through modesty, delicacy, generosity, refinement of soul.'

His forbearance to Godwin, to Godwin lectur-
ing and renouncing him and at the same time
holding out, as I have said, his hat to him for
alms, is wonderful ; but the dignity with which
he at last, in a letter perfect for propriety of tone,
reads a lesson to his ignoble father-in-law, is in
the best possible style :—

'Perhaps it is well that you should be informed that I consider your last letter to be written in a style of haughtiness and encroachment which neither awes nor imposes on me ; but I have no desire to transgress the limits which you place to our intercourse, nor in any future instance will I make any remarks but such as arise from the strict question in discussion.'

And again :—

'My astonishment, and, I will confess, when I have been treated with most harshness and cruelty by you, my indignation, has been extreme, that, knowing as you do my nature, any considerations should have prevailed on you to have been thus harsh and cruel. I lamented also over my ruined hopes of all that your genius once taught me to expect from your virtue, when I found that for yourself, your family, and your creditors, you would submit to that communication with me which you once rejected and abhorred, and which no pity for my poverty or sufferings, assumed willingly for you, could avail to extort.'

Moreover, though Shelley has no humour, he can show as quick and sharp a tact as the most practised man of the world. He has been with Byron and the Countess Guiccioli, and he writes of the latter :—

'La Guiccioli is a very pretty, sentimental, innocent Italian, who has sacrificed an immense future for
the sake of Lord Byron, and who, if I know anything of my friend, of her, and of human nature, will
hereafter have plenty of opportunity to repent her
rashness.'

Tact also, and something better than tact, he
shows in his dealings, in order to befriend Leigh
Hunt, with Lord Byron. He writes to Hunt :—

'Particular circumstances, or rather, I should say,
particular dispositions in Lord Byron's character,
render the close and exclusive intimacy with him, in
which I find myself, intolerable to me; thus much,
my best friend, I will confess and confide to you.
No feelings of my own shall injure or interfere with
what is now nearest to them—your interest ; and I
will take care to preserve the little influence I may
have over this Proteus, in whom such strange ex-
tremes are reconciled, until we meet.'

And so we have come back again, at last, to
our original Shelley—to the Shelley of the lovely
and well-known picture, to the Shelley with
'flushed, feminine, artless face,' the Shelley ' blush-
ing like a girl,' of Trelawny. Professor Dowden

gives us some further attempts at portraiture. One by a Miss Rose, of Shelley at Marlow :—

'He was the most interesting figure I ever saw ; his eyes like a deer's, bright but rather wild ; his white throat unfettered ; his slender but to me almost faultless shape ; his brown long coat with curling lambs' wool collar and cuffs—in fact, his whole appearance—are as fresh in my recollection as an occurrence of yesterday.'

Feminine enthusiasm may be deemed suspicious, but a Captain Kennedy must surely be able to keep his head. Captain Kennedy was quartered at Horsham in 1813, and saw Shelley when he was on a stolen visit, in his father's absence, at Field Place :—

'He received me with frankness and kindliness, as if he had known me from childhood, and at once won my heart. I fancy I see him now as he sate by the window, and hear his voice, the tones of which impressed me with his sincerity and simplicity. His resemblance to his sister Elizabeth was as striking as if they had been twins. His eyes were most expressive ; his complexion beautifully fair, his features exquisitely fine ; his hair was dark, and no peculiar attention to its arrangement was manifest. In person he was slender and gentlemanlike, but inclined to stoop ; his gait was decidedly not military. The general appearance indicated great delicacy of constitution. One would at once pronounce of him that he was different from other men. There was an earnestness in his manner and such perfect gentleness of breeding and freedom from everything artificial as charmed every one. I never met a man who so immediately won upon me.'

Mrs. Gisborne's son, who knew Shelley well at Leghorn, declared Captain Kennedy's description of him to be ' the best and most truthful I have ever seen.'

To all this we have to add the charm of the man's writings—of Shelley's poetry. It is his poetry, above everything else, which for many people establishes that he is an angel. Of his poetry I have not space now to speak. But let no one suppose that a want of humour and a self-delusion such as Shelley's have no effect upon a man's poetry. The man Shelley, in very truth, is not entirely sane, and Shelley's poetry is not entirely sane either. The Shelley of actual life is a vision of beauty and radiance, indeed, but availing

nothing, effecting nothing. And in poetry, no
less than in life, he is 'a beautiful *and ineffectual*
angel, beating in the void his luminous wings in
vain.'

VIII

COUNT LEO TOLSTOI[1]

IN reviewing at the time of its first publication, thirty years ago, Flaubert's remarkable novel of *Madame Bovary*, Sainte-Beuve observed that in Flaubert we come to another manner, another kind of inspiration, from those which had prevailed hitherto; we find ourselves dealing, he said, with a man of a new and different generation from novelists like George Sand. The ideal has ceased, the lyric vein is dried up; the new men are cured of lyricism and the ideal; 'a severe and pitiless truth has made its entry, as the last word of experience, even into art itself.' The characters of the new literature of fiction are 'science,

1 Published in the *Fortnightly Review*, December 1887.

a spirit of observation, maturity, force, a touch of hardness.' *L'idéal a cessé, le lyrique a tari.*

The spirit of observation and the touch of hardness (let us retain these mild and inoffensive terms) have since been carried in the French novel very far. So far have they been carried, indeed, that in spite of the advantage which the French language, familiar to the cultivated classes everywhere, confers on the French novel, this novel has lost much of its attraction for those classes; it no longer commands their attention as it did formerly. The famous English novelists have passed away, and have left no successors of like fame. It is not the English novel, therefore, which has inherited the vogue lost by the French novel. It is the novel of a country new to literature, or at any rate unregarded, till lately, by the general public of readers : it is the novel of Russia. The Russian novel has now the vogue, and deserves to have it. If fresh literary productions maintain this vogue and enhance it, we shall all be learning Russian.

The Slav nature, or at any rate the Russian nature, the Russian nature as it shows itself in the Russian novels, seems marked by an extreme sensitiveness, a consciousness most quick and acute both for what the man's self is experiencing, and also for what others in contact with him are thinking and feeling. In a nation full of life, but young, and newly in contact with an old and powerful civilisation, this sensitiveness and self-consciousness are prompt to appear. In the Americans, as well as in the Russians, we see them active in a high degree. They are somewhat agitating and disquieting agents to their possessor, but they have, if they get fair play, great powers for evoking and enriching a literature. But the Americans, as we know, are apt to set them at rest in the manner of my friend Colonel Higginson of Boston. 'As I take it, Nature said, some years since: "Thus far the English is my best race; but we have had Englishmen enough; we need something with a little more buoyancy than the Englishman; let us lighten the structure, even

at some peril in the process. Put in one drop
more of nervous fluid, and make the American."
With that drop, a new range of promise opened on
the human race, and a lighter, finer, more highly
organised type of mankind was born.'   People
who by this sort of thing give rest to their sensitive and busy self-consciousness may very well, perhaps, be on their way to great material prosperity,
to great political power; but they are scarcely on
the right way to a great literature, a serious art.

The Russian does not assuage his sensitiveness
in this fashion.   The Russian man of letters does
not make Nature say: 'The Russian is my best
race.'   He finds relief to his sensitiveness in
letting his perceptions have perfectly free play,
and in recording their reports with perfect fidelity.
The sincereness with which the reports are given
has even something childlike and touching.   In
the novel of which I am going to speak there is not
a line, not a trait, brought in for the glorification
of Russia, or to feed vanity ; things and characters
go as nature takes them, and the author is absorbed

in seeing how nature takes them and in relating it. But we have here a condition of things which is highly favourable to the production of good literature, of good art. We have great sensitiveness, subtlety, and finesse, addressing themselves with entire disinterestedness and simplicity to the representation of human life. The Russian novelist is thus master of a spell to which the secrets of human nature—both what is external and what is internal, gesture and manner no less than thought and feeling—willingly make themselves known. The crown of literature is poetry, and the Russians have not yet had a great poet. But in that form of imaginative literature which in our day is the most popular and the most possible, the Russians at the present moment seem to me to hold, as Mr. Gladstone would say, the field. They have great novelists, and of one of their great novelists I wish now to speak.

Count Leo Tolstoi is about sixty years old, and tells us that he shall write novels no more. He is now occupied with religion and with the Chris-

tian life. His writings concerning these great
matters are not allowed, I believe, to obtain publication in Russia, but instalments of them in
French and English reach us from time to time.
I find them very interesting, but I find his novel
of *Anna Karénine* more interesting still. I believe that many readers prefer to *Anna Karénine*
Count Tolstoi's other great novel, *La Guerre et la
Paix*. But in the novel one prefers, I think, to
have the novelist dealing with the life which he
knows from having lived it, rather than with the
life which he knows from books or hearsay. If
one has to choose a representative work of Thack-
eray, it is *Vanity Fair* which one would take
rather than *The Virginians*. In like manner I
take *Anna Karénine* as the novel best represent-
ing Count Tolstoi. I use the French translation;
in general, as I long ago said, work of this kind is
better done in France than in England, and *Anna
Karénine* is perhaps also a novel which goes better
into French than into English, just as Frederika
Bremer's *Home* goes into English better than into

French. After I have done with *Anna Karénine*
I must say something of Count Tolstoi's religious
writings. Of these too I use the French translation, so far as it is available. The English translation, however, which came into my hands late,
seems to be in general clear and good. Let me
say in passing that it has neither the same arrangement, nor the same titles, nor altogether the same
contents, with the French translation.

There are many characters in *Anna Karénine*—
too many if we look in it for a work of art in
which the action shall be vigorously one, and to
that one action everything shall converge. There
are even two main actions extending throughout
the book, and we keep passing from one of them
to the other — from the affairs of Anna and
Wronsky to the affairs of Kitty and Levine.
People appear in connection with these two main
actions whose appearance and proceedings do not
in the least contribute to develop them; incidents are multiplied which we expect are to lead
to something important, but which do not. What,

for instance, does the episode of Kitty's friend
Warinka and Levine's brother Serge Ivanitch,
their inclination for one another and its failure to
come to anything, contribute to the development
of either the character or the fortunes of Kitty
and Levine ? What does the incident of Levine's
long delay in getting to church to be married, a
delay which as we read of it seems to have significance, really import ? It turns out to import
absolutely nothing, and to be introduced solely to
give the author the pleasure of telling us that
all Levine's shirts had been packed up.

But the truth is we are not to take *Anna
Karénine* as a work of art; we are to take it as
a piece of life. A piece of life it is. The author
has not invented and combined it, he has seen it ;
it has all happened before his inward eye, and it
was in this wise that it happened. Levine's shirts
were packed up, and he was late for his wedding
in consequence ; Warinka and Serge Ivanitch met
at Levine's country-house and went out walking
together ; Serge was very near proposing, but did

not. The author saw it all happening so—saw it, and therefore relates it; and what his novel in this way loses in art it gains in reality.

For this is the result which, by his extra-ordinary fineness of perception, and by his sincere fidelity to it, the author achieves; he works in us a sense of the absolute reality of his personages and their doings. Anna's shoulders, and masses of hair, and half-shut eyes; Alexis Karénine's up-drawn eyebrows, and tired smile, and cracking finger-joints; Stiva's eyes suffused with facile moisture—these are as real to us as any of those outward peculiarities which in our own circle of acquaintance we are noticing daily, while the inner man of our own circle of acquaintance, happily or unhappily, lies a great deal less clearly revealed to us than that of Count Tolstoi's crea-tions.

I must speak of only a few of these creations, the chief personages and no more. The book opens with 'Stiva,' and who that has once made Stiva's acquaintance will ever forget him? We

are living, in Count Tolstoi's novel, among the
great people of Moscow and St. Petersburg, the
nobles and the high functionaries, the governing
class of Russia. Stépane Arcadiévitch—'Stiva'
—is Prince Oblonsky, and descended from Rurik,
although to think of him as anything except
'Stiva' is difficult. His *air souriant*, his good
looks, his satisfaction; his 'ray,' which made the
Tartar waiter at the club joyful in contemplating
it; his pleasure in oysters and champagne, his
pleasure in making people happy and in rendering services; his need of money, his attachment to
the French governess, his distress at his wife's
distress, his affection for her and the children;
his emotion and suffused eyes, while he quite dis-
misses the care of providing funds for household
expenses and education ; and the French attachment, contritely given up to-day only to be succeeded by some other attachment to-morrow—no
never, certainly, shall we come to forget Stiva.
Anna, the heroine, is Stiva's sister. His wife
Dolly (these English diminutives are common

among Count Tolstoi's ladies) is daughter of
the Prince and Princess Cherbatzky, grandees
who show us Russian high life by its most respectable side; the Prince, in particular, is excellent
—simple, sensible, right-feeling; a man of dignity
and honour. His daughters, Dolly and Kitty,
are charming. Dolly, Stiva's wife, is sorely tried
by her husband, full of anxieties for the children, with no money to spend on them or herself,
poorly dressed, worn and aged before her time.
She has moments of despairing doubt whether the
gay people may not be after all in the right,
whether virtue and principle answer; whether
happiness does not dwell with adventuresses and
profligates, brilliant and perfectly dressed adventuresses and profligates, in a land flowing with
roubles and champagne. But in a quarter of an
hour she comes right again and is herself—a nature
straight, honest, faithful, loving, sound to the core;
such she is and such she remains; she can be
no other. Her sister Kitty is at bottom of the
same temper, but she has her experience to get,

while Dolly, when the book begins, has already acquired hers.   Kitty is adored by Levine, in whom we are told that many traits are to be found of the character and history of Count Tolstoi himself.   Levine belongs to the world of great people by his birth and property, but he is not at all a man of the world.   He has been a reader and thinker, he has a conscience, he has public spirit and would ameliorate the condition of the people, he lives on his estate in the country, and occupies himself zealously with local business, schools, and agriculture.   But he is shy, apt to suspect and to take offence, somewhat impracticable, out of his element in the gay world of Moscow.   Kitty likes him, but her fancy has been taken by a brilliant guardsman, Count Wronsky, who has paid her attentions. Wronsky is described to us by Stiva; he is 'one of the finest specimens of the *jeunesse dorée* of St. Petersburg ; immensely rich, handsome, aide-de-camp to the emperor, great interest at his back, and a good fellow notwithstanding ; more than a good fellow, intelligent besides and well read—a man who has a splendid career before him.' Let us complete the picture by adding that Wronsky is a powerful man, over thirty, bald at the top of his head, with irreproachable manners, cool and calm, but a little haughty. A hero, one murmurs to oneself, too much of the Guy Livingstone type, though without the bravado and exaggeration. And such is, justly enough perhaps, the first impression, an impression which continues all through the first volume; but Wronsky, as we shall see, improves towards the end.

Kitty discourages Levine, who retires in misery and confusion. But Wronsky is attracted by Anna Karénine, and ceases his attentions to Kitty. The impression made on her heart by Wronsky was not deep; but she is so keenly mortified with herself, so ashamed, and so upset, that she falls ill, and is sent with her family to winter abroad. There she regains health and mental composure, and discovers at the same time that her liking for Levine was deeper than she knew, that it was a genuine feeling, a strong and lasting one.

On her return they meet, their hearts come together, they are married ; and in spite of Levine's
waywardness, irritability, and unsettlement of
mind, of which I shall have more to say presently,
they are profoundly happy. Well, and who could
help being happy with Kitty ? So I find myself
adding impatiently. Count Tolstoi's heroines are
really so living and charming that one takes them,
fiction though they are, too seriously.

But the interest of the book centres in Anna
Karénine. She is Stiva's sister, married to a high
official at St. Petersburg, Alexis Karénine. She
has been married to him nine years, and has one
child, a boy named Serge. The marriage had not
brought happiness to her, she had found in it no
satisfaction to her heart and soul, she had a sense
of want and isolation ; but she is devoted to her
boy, occupied, calm. The charm of her personality
is felt even before she appears, from the moment
when we hear of her being sent for as the good
angel to reconcile Dolly with Stiva. Then she
arrives at the Moscow station from St. Peters-

burg, and we see the gray eyes with their long eye-
lashes, the graceful carriage, the gentle and caress-
ing smile on the fresh lips, the vivacity restrained
but waiting to break through, the fulness of life,
the softness and strength joined, the harmony, the
bloom, the charm. She goes to Dolly, and achieves,
with infinite tact and tenderness, the task of re-
conciliation. At a ball a few days later, we add
to our first impression of Anna's beauty, dark hair,
a quantity of little curls over her temples and at
the back of her neck, sculptural shoulders, firm
throat, and beautiful arms. She is in a plain dress
of black velvet with a pearl necklace, a bunch of
forget-me-nots in the front of her dress, another in
her hair. This is Anna Karénine.

She had travelled from St. Petersburg with
Wronsky's mother; had seen him at the Moscow
station, where he came to meet his mother, had
been struck with his looks and manner, and
touched by his behaviour in an accident which
happened while they were in the station to a poor
workman crushed by a train. At the ball she

meets him again ; she is fascinated by him and he
by her. She had been told of Kitty's fancy, and
had gone to the ball meaning to help Kitty ; but
Kitty is forgotten, or at any rate neglected ; the
spell which draws Wronsky and Anna is irresistible. Kitty finds herself opposite to them in a
quadrille together :—

> ' She seemed to remark in Anna the symptoms
> of an over-excitement which she herself knew from
> experience—that of success. Anna appeared to her
> as if intoxicated with it. Kitty knew to what to
> attribute that brilliant and animated look, that
> happy and triumphant smile, those half-parted lips,
> those movements full of grace and harmony.'

Anna returns to St. Petersburg, and Wronsky
returns there at the same time ; they meet on the
journey, they keep meeting in society, and Anna
begins to find her husband, who before had not
been sympathetic, intolerable. Alexis Karénine
is much older than herself, a bureaucrat, a formalist,
a poor creature; he has conscience, there is a root of
goodness in him, but on the surface and until deeply
stirred he is tiresome, pedantic, vain, exasperating.

The change in Anna is not in the slightest degree comprehended by him ; he sees nothing which an intelligent man might in such a case see, and does nothing which an intelligent man would do. Anna abandons herself to her passion for Wronsky.

I remember M. Nisard saying to me many years ago at the École Normale in Paris, that he respected the English because they are *une nation qui sait se gêner*—people who can put constraint on themselves and go through what is disagreeable. Perhaps in the Slav nature this valuable faculty is somewhat wanting ; a very strong impulse is too much regarded as irresistible, too little as what can be resisted and ought to be resisted, however difficult and disagreeable the resistance may be. In our high society with its pleasure and dissipation, laxer notions may to some extent prevail ; but in general an English mind will be startled by Anna's suffering herself to be so overwhelmed and irretrievably carried away by her passion, by her almost at once regarding it, apparently, as something which it was hopeless to fight against. And this I say irrespectively of the worth of her lover. Wronsky's gifts and graces hardly qualify him, one might think, to be the object of so instantaneous and mighty a passion on the part of a woman like Anna. But that is not the question. Let us allow that these passions are incalculable; let us allow that one of the male sex scarcely does justice, perhaps, to the powerful and handsome guardsman and his attractions. But if Wronsky had been even such a lover as Alcibiades or the Master of Ravenswood, still that Anna, being what she is and her circumstances being what they are, should show not a hope, hardly a thought, of conquering her passion, of escaping from its fatal power, is to our notions strange and a little bewildering.

I state the objection; let me add that it is the triumph of Anna's charm that it remains paramount for us nevertheless; that throughout her course, with its failures, errors, and miseries, still the impression of her large, fresh, rich, generous, delightful nature, never leaves us—keeps our sympathy, keeps even, I had almost said, our respect.

To return to the story. Soon enough poor Anna begins to experience the truth of what the Wise Man told us long ago, that 'the way of transgressors is hard.' Her agitation at a steeple-chase where Wronsky is in danger attracts her husband's notice and provokes his remonstrance. He is bitter and contemptuous. In a transport of passion Anna declares to him that she is his wife no longer ; that she loves Wronsky, belongs to Wronsky. Hard at first, formal, cruel, thinking only of himself, Karénine, who, as I have said, has a conscience, is touched by grace at the moment when Anna's troubles reach their height. He returns to her to find her with a child just born to her and Wronsky, the lover in the house and Anna apparently dying. Karénine has words of kindness and forgiveness only. The noble and victorious effort transfigures him, and all that her husband gains in the eyes of Anna, her lover Wronsky loses. Wronsky comes to Anna's bed-

side, and standing there by Karénine, buries his
face in his hands. Anna says to him, in the
hurried voice of fever :—

'"Uncover your face; look at that man; he is
a saint. Yes, uncover your face; uncover it," she
repeated with an angry air. "Alexis, uncover his
face; I want to see him."

'Alexis took the hands of Wronsky and un-
covered his face, disfigured by suffering and humilia-
tion.

'"Give him your hand; pardon him."

'Alexis stretched out his hand without even
seeking to restrain his tears.

'"Thank God, thank God !" she said; "all
is ready now. How ugly those flowers are," she
went on, pointing to the wall-paper; "they are not
a bit like violets. My God, my God ! when will all
this end ? Give me morphine, doctor—I want morphine. Oh, my God, my God ! "'

She seems dying, and Wronsky rushes out and
shoots himself. And so, in a common novel, the
story would end. Anna would die, Wronsky
would commit suicide, Karénine would survive,
in possession of our admiration and sympathy.
But the story does not always end so in life :

neither does it end so in Count Tolstoi's novel.
Anna recovers from her fever, Wronsky from his
wound. Anna's passion for Wronsky reawakens,
her estrangement from Karénine returns. Nor
does Karénine remain at the height at which in
the forgiveness scene we saw him. He is formal,
pedantic, irritating. Alas! even if he were not
all these, perhaps even his *pince-nez*, and his rising
eyebrows, and his cracking finger-joints, would
have been provocation enough. Anna and Wronsky depart together. They stay for a time in
Italy, then return to Russia. But her position is
false, her disquietude incessant, and happiness is
impossible for her. She takes opium every night,
only to find that 'not poppy nor mandragora shall
ever medicine her to that sweet sleep which she
owed yesterday.' Jealousy and irritability grow
upon her ; she tortures Wronsky, she tortures
herself. Under these trials Wronsky, it must be
said, comes out well, and rises in our esteem.
His love for Anna endures ; he behaves, as our
English phrase is, 'like a gentleman'; his patience

T

is in general exemplary. But then Anna, let us remember, is to the last, through all the fret and misery, still Anna; always with something which charms; nay, with something, even, something in her nature, which consoles and does good. Her life, however, was becoming impossible under its existing conditions. A trifling misunderstanding brought the inevitable end. After a quarrel with Anna, Wronsky had gone one morning into the country to see his mother; Anna summons him by telegraph to return at once, and receives an answer from him that he cannot return before ten at night. She follows him to his mother's place in the country, and at the station hears what leads her to believe that he is not coming back. Maddened with jealousy and misery, she descends the platform and throws herself under the wheels of a goods train passing through the station. It is over—the graceful head is untouched, but all the rest is a crushed, formless heap. Poor Anna!

We have been in a world which misconducts

itself nearly as much as the world of a French novel all palpitating with 'modernity.' But there are two things in which the Russian novel—Count Tolstoi's novel at any rate—is very advantageously distinguished from the type of novel now so much in request in France. In the first place, there is no fine sentiment, at once tiresome and false. We are not told to believe, for example, that Anna is wonderfully exalted and ennobled by her passion for Wronsky. The English reader is thus saved from many a groan of impatience. The other thing is yet more important. Our Russian novelist deals abundantly with criminal passion and with adultery, but he does not seem to feel himself owing any service to the goddess Lubricity, or bound to put in touches at this goddess's dictation. Much in *Anna Karénine* is painful, much is unpleasant, but nothing is of a nature to trouble the senses, or to please those who wish their senses troubled. This taint is wholly absent. In the French novels where it is so abundantly present its baneful effects do not end with itself. Burns long ago remarked with deep truth that it *petrifies feeling*. Let us revert for a moment to the powerful novel of which I spoke at the outset, *Madame Bovary*. Undoubtedly the taint in question is present in *Madame Bovary*, although to a much less degree than in more recent French novels, which will be in every one's mind. But *Madame Bovary*, with this taint, is a work of *petrified feeling*; over it hangs an atmosphere of bitterness, irony, impotence; not a personage in the book to rejoice or console us; the springs of freshness and feeling are not there to create such personages. Emma Bovary follows a course in some respects like that of Anna, but where, in Emma Bovary, is Anna's charm? The treasures of compassion, tenderness, insight, which alone, amid such guilt and misery, can enable charm to subsist and to emerge, are wanting to Flaubert. He is cruel, with the cruelty of petrified feeling, to his poor heroine; he pursues her without pity or pause, as with malignity; he is harder upon her himself than any reader even, I think, will be inclined to be.

But where the springs of feeling have carried Count Tolstoi, since he created Anna ten or twelve years ago, we have now to see.

We must return to Constantine Dmitrich Levine. Levine, as I have already said, thinks. Between the age of twenty and that of thirty-five he had lost, he tells us, the Christian belief in which he had been brought up, a loss of which examples nowadays abound certainly everywhere, but which in Russia, as in France, is among all young men of the upper and cultivated classes more a matter of course, perhaps, more universal, more avowed, than it is with us. Levine had adopted the scientific notions current all round him; talked of cells, organisms, the indestructibility of matter, the conservation of force, and was of opinion, with his comrades of the university, that religion no longer existed. But he was of a serious nature, and the question what his life meant, whence it came, whither it tended, presented themselves to him in moments of crisis and affliction with irresistible importunity, and getting no answer, haunted him, tortured him, made him think of suicide.

Two things, meanwhile, he noticed. One was, that he and his university friends had been mistaken in supposing that Christian belief no longer existed; they had lost it, but they were not all the world. Levine observed that the persons to whom he was most attached, his own wife Kitty amongst the number, retained it and drew comfort from it; that the women generally, and almost the whole of the Russian common people, retained it and drew comfort from it. The other was, that his scientific friends, though not troubled like himself by questionings about the meaning of human life, were untroubled by such questionings, not because they had got an answer to them, but because, entertaining themselves intellectually with the consideration of the cell theory, and evolution, and the indestructibility of matter, and the conservation of force, and the like, they were satisfied with this entertainment, and did not perplex themselves with investigating the meaning and object of their own life at all.

But Levine noticed further that he himself did not actually proceed to commit suicide; on the contrary, he lived on his lands as his father had done before him, busied himself with all the duties of his station, married Kitty, was delighted when a son was born to him. Nevertheless he was indubitably not happy at bottom, restless and disquieted, his disquietude sometimes amounting to agony.

Now on one of his bad days he was in the field with his peasants, and one of them happened to say to him, in answer to a question from Levine why one farmer should in a certain case act more humanely than another: 'Men are not all alike; one man lives for his belly, like Mitiovuck, another for his soul, for God, like old Plato.'[1]—'What do you call,' cried Levine, 'living for his soul, for God?' The peasant answered: 'It's quite simple —living by the rule of God, of the truth. All

[1] A common name among Russian peasants.

men are not the same, that's certain. You yourself, for instance, Constantine Dmitrich, you
wouldn't do wrong by a poor man.' Levine
gave no answer, but turned away with the phrase,
living by the rule of God, of the truth, sounding in
his ears.

Then he reflected that he had been born of
parents professing this rule, as their parents again
had professed it before them ; that he had sucked
it in with his mother's milk ; that some sense of
it, some strength and nourishment from it, had
been ever with him although he knew it not ;
that if he had tried to do the duties of his station
it was by help of the secret support ministered by
this rule ; that if in his moments of despairing
restlessness and agony, when he was driven to
think of suicide, he had yet not committed suicide,
it was because this rule had silently enabled him
to do his duty in some degree, and had given
him some hold upon life and happiness in consequence.

The words came to him as a clue of which he

could never again lose sight, and which with full
consciousness and strenuous endeavour he must
henceforth follow.   He sees his nephews and
nieces throwing their milk at one another and
scolded by Dolly for it.   He says to himself that
these children are wasting their subsistence because they have not to earn it for themselves and
do not know its value, and he exclaims inwardly :
'I, a Christian, brought up in the faith, my life
filled with the benefits of Christianity, living
on these benefits without being conscious of it, I,
like these children, I have been trying to destroy
what makes and builds up my life.'   But now
the feeling has been borne in upon him, clear
and precious, that what he has to do is to *be
good ;* he has 'cried to *Him.*'   What will come
of it ?

'I shall probably continue to get out of temper
with my coachman, to go into useless arguments, to
air my ideas unseasonably ; I shall always feel a
barrier between the sanctuary of my soul and the
soul of other people, even that of my wife ; I shall
always be holding her responsible for my annoyances

and feeling sorry for it directly afterwards. I shall
continue to pray without being able to explain to
myself why I pray ; but my inner life has won its
liberty ; it will no longer be at the mercy of events,
and every minute of my existence will have a
meaning sure and profound which it will be in my
power to impress on every single one of my actions,
that of *being good.*'

With these words the novel of *Anna Karénine*
ends. But in Levine's religious experiences Count
Tolstoi was relating his own, and the history is
continued in three autobiographical works translated from him, which have within the last two
or three years been published in Paris : *Ma Confession, Ma Religion,* and *Que Faire.* Our author
announces further, 'two great works,' on which he
has spent six years : one a criticism of dogmatic
theology, the other a new translation of the four
Gospels, with a concordance of his own arranging.
The results which he claims to have established in
these two works, are, however, indicated sufficiently in the three published volumes which I
have named above.

These autobiographical volumes show the same extraordinary penetration, the same perfect sincerity, which are exhibited in the author's novel. As autobiography they are of profound interest, and they are full, moreover, of acute and fruitful remarks. I have spoken of the advantages which the Russian genius possesses for imaginative literature. Perhaps for Biblical exegesis, for the criticism of religion and its documents, the advantage lies more with the older nations of the West. They will have more of the experience, width of knowledge, patience, sobriety, requisite for these studies; they may probably be less impulsive, less heady.

Count Tolstoi regards the change accomplished in himself during the last half-dozen years, he regards his recent studies and the ideas which he has acquired through them, as epoch-making in his life and of capital importance :—

'Five years ago faith came to me ; I believed in the doctrine of Jesus, and all my life suddenly changed. I ceased to desire that which previously I desired, and, on the other hand, I took to desiring what I had never desired before. That which formerly used to appear good in my eyes appeared evil, that which used to appear evil appeared good.'

The novel of *Anna Karénine* belongs to that past which Count Tolstoi has left behind him; his new studies and the works founded on them are what is important; light and salvation are there. Yet I will venture to express my doubt whether these works contain, as their contribution to the cause of religion and to the establishment of the true mind and message of Jesus, much that had not already been given or indicated by Count Tolstoi in relating, in *Anna Karénine*, Levine's mental history. Points raised in that history are developed and enforced; there is an abundant and admirable exhibition of knowledge of human nature, penetrating insight, fearless sincerity, wit, sarcasm, eloquence, style. And we have too the direct autobiography of a man not only interesting to us from his soul and talent, but highly interesting also from his nationality, position, and course of proceeding. But to light and salvation in the Christian religion we are not, I think, brought

very much nearer than in Levine's history. I
ought to add that what was already present in that
history seems to me of high importance and value.
Let us see what it amounts to.

I must be general and I must be brief; neither
my limits nor my purpose permit the introduction
of what is abstract.   But in Count Tolstoi's religious philosophy there is very little which is
abstract, arid.   The idea of *life* is his master idea
in studying and establishing religion.   He speaks
impatiently of St. Paul as a source, in common
with the Fathers and the Reformers, of that ecclesiastical theology which misses the essential and
fails to present Christ's Gospel aright.   Yet Paul's
' law of the spirit of life in Christ Jesus freeing me
from the law of sin and death ' is the pith and
ground of all Count Tolstoi's theology.   Moral life
is the gift of God, is God, and this true life, this
union with God to which we aspire, we reach
through Jesus.   We reach it through union with
Jesus and by adopting his life.   This doctrine is
proved true for us by the life in God, to be acquired

through Jesus, being what our nature feels after and moves to, by the warning of misery if we are severed from it, the sanction of happiness if we find it. Of the access for *us*, at any rate, to the spirit of life, us who are born in Christendom, are in touch, conscious or unconscious, with Christianity, this is the true account. Questions over which the churches spend so much labour and time—questions about the Trinity, about the godhead of Christ, about the procession of the Holy Ghost, are not vital; what is vital is the doctrine of access to the spirit of life through Jesus.

Sound and saving doctrine, in my opinion, this is. It may be gathered in a great degree from what Count Tolstoi had already given us in the novel of *Anna Karénine*. But of course it is greatly developed in the special works which have followed. Many of these developments are, I will repeat, of striking force, interest, and value. In *Anna Karénine* we had been told of the scepticism of the upper and educated classes in Russia

But what reality is added by such an anecdote as the following from *Ma Confession* :—

'I remember that when I was about eleven years old we had a visit one Sunday from a boy, since dead, who announced to my brother and me, as great news, a discovery just made at his public school. This discovery was to the effect that God had no existence, and that everything which we were taught about Him was pure invention.'

Count Tolstoi touched, in *Anna Karénine*, on the failure of science to tell a man what his life means. Many a sharp stroke does he add in his latter writings :—

'Development is going on, and there are laws which guide it. You yourself are a part of the whole. Having come to understand the whole so far as is possible, and having comprehended the law of development, you will comprehend also your place in that whole, you will understand yourself.

'In spite of all the shame the confession costs me, there was a time, I declare, when I tried to look as if I was satisfied with this sort of thing !'

But the men of science may take comfort from hearing that Count Tolstoi treats the men of letters

no better than them, although he is a man of letters
himself :—

'The judgment which my literary companions
passed on life was to the effect that life in general
is in a state of progress, and that in this development we, the men of letters, take the principal part.
The vocation of us artists and poets is to instruct the
world ; and to prevent my coming out with the
natural question, "What am I, and what am I to
teach ?" it was explained to me that it was useless to
know that, and that the artist and the poet taught
without perceiving how. I passed for a superb artist,
a great poet, and consequently it was but natural
I should appropriate this theory. I, the artist, the
poet—I wrote, I taught, without myself knowing
what. I was paid for what I did. I had everything :
splendid fare and lodging, women, society ; I had
la gloire. Consequently, what I taught was very
good. This faith in the importance of poetry and of
the development of life was a religion, and I was
one of its priests—a very agreeable and advantageous
office.

'And I lived ever so long in this belief, never
doubting but that it was true !'

The adepts of this literary and scientific religion
are not numerous, to be sure, in comparison with
the mass of the people, and the mass of the people,

as Levine had remarked, find comfort still in the old religion of Christendom; but of the mass of the people our literary and scientific instructors make no account. Like Solomon and Schopenhauer, these gentlemen, and 'society' along with them, are, moreover, apt to say that life is, after all, vanity : but then they all know of no life except their own.

'It used to appear to me that the small number of cultivated, rich, and idle men, of whom I was one, composed the whole of humanity, and that the millions and millions of other men who had lived and are still living were not in reality men at all. Incomprehensible as it now seems to me, that I should have gone on considering life without seeing the life which was surrounding me on all sides, the life of humanity; strange as it is to think that I should have been so mistaken, and have fancied my life, the life of the Solomons and the Schopenhauers, to be the veritable and normal life, while the life of the masses was but a matter of no importance — strangely odd as this seems to me now, so it was, notwithstanding.'

And this pretentious minority, who call themselves 'society,' 'the world,' and to whom their

own life, the life of 'the world,' seems the only life
worth naming, are all the while miserable! Our
author found it so in his own experience :—

'In my life, an exceptionally happy one from a
worldly point of view, I can number such a quantity
of sufferings endured for the sake of "the world,"
that they would be enough to furnish a martyr for
Jesus. All the most painful passages in my life,
beginning with the orgies and duels of my student
days, the wars I have been in, the illnesses, and the
abnormal and unbearable conditions in which I am
living now—all this is but one martyrdom endured
in the name of the doctrine of the world. Yes, and I
speak of my own life, exceptionally happy from the
world's point of view.

'Let any sincere man pass his life in review, and
he will perceive that never, not once, has he suffered
through practising the doctrine of Jesus; the chief
part of the miseries of his life have proceeded solely
from his following, contrary to his inclination, the
spell of the doctrine of the world.'

On the other hand, the simple, the multitudes
outside of this spell, are comparatively contented :—

'In opposition to what I saw in our circle, where

life without faith is possible, and where I doubt whether one in a thousand would confess himself a believer, I conceive that among the people (in Russia) there is not one sceptic to many thousands of believers. Just contrary to what I saw in our circle, where life passes in idleness, amusements, and discontent with life, I saw that of these men of the people the whole life was passed in severe labour, and yet they were contented with life. Instead of complaining like the persons in our world of the hardship of their lot, these poor people received sickness and disappointments without any revolt, without opposition, but with a firm and tranquil confidence that so it was to be, that it could not be otherwise, and that it was all right.'

All this is but development, sometimes rather surprising, but always powerful and interesting, of what we have already had in the pages of *Anna Karénine*. And like Levine in that novel, Count Tolstoi was driven by his inward struggle and misery very near to suicide. What is new in the recent books is the solution and cure announced. Levine had accepted a provisional solution of the difficulties oppressing him; he had lived right on, so to speak, obeying his conscience, but not asking how far all his actions hung together and were consistent :—

'He advanced money to a peasant to get him out of the clutches of a money-lender, but did not give up the arrears due to himself; he punished thefts of wood strictly, but would have scrupled to impound a peasant's cattle trespassing on his fields; he did not pay the wages of a labourer whose father's death caused him to leave work in the middle of harvest, but he pensioned and maintained his old servants; he let his peasants wait while he went to give his wife a kiss after he came home, but would not have made them wait while he went to visit his bees.'

Count Tolstoi has since advanced to a far more definite and stringent rule of life—the positive doctrine, he thinks, of Jesus. It is the determination and promulgation of this rule which is the novelty in our author's recent works. He extracts this essential doctrine, or rule of Jesus, from the Sermon on the Mount, and presents it in a body of commandments—Christ's commandments; the pith, he says, of the New Testament, as the Decalogue is the pith of the Old. These all-important commandments of Christ are 'commandments of peace,' and five in number. The first commandment is : 'Live in peace with all men ; treat no one as contemptible and beneath you. Not only allow yourself no anger, but do not rest until you have dissipated even unreasonable anger in others against yourself.' The second is : 'No libertinage and no divorce ; let every man have one wife and every woman one husband.' The third : 'Never on any pretext take an oath of service of any kind ; all such oaths are imposed for a bad purpose.' The fourth : 'Never employ force against the evil-doer; bear whatever wrong is done to you without opposing the wrongdoer or seeking to have him punished.' The fifth and last : 'Renounce all distinction of nationality ; do not admit that men of another nation may ever be treated by you as enemies ; love all men alike as alike near to you ; do good to all alike.'

If these five commandments were generally observed, says Count Tolstoi, all men would become

brothers. Certainly the actual society in which
we live would be changed and dissolved. Armies
and wars would be renounced; courts of justice,
police, property, would be renounced also. And
whatever the rest of us may do, Count Tolstoi at
least will do his duty and follow Christ's commandments sincerely. He has given up rank,
office, and property, and earns his bread by the
labour of his own hands. 'I believe in Christ's
commandments,' he says, 'and this faith changes
my whole former estimate of what is good and
great, bad and low, in human life.' At present—

'Everything which I used to think bad and low—
the rusticity of the peasant, the plainness of lodging,
food, clothing, manners—all this has become good
and great in my eyes. At present I can no longer
contribute to anything which raises me externally
above others, which separates me from them. I
cannot, as formerly, recognise either in my own
case or in that of others any title, rank, or quality
beyond the title and quality of man. I cannot seek
fame and praise ; I cannot seek a culture which
separates me from men. I cannot refrain from
seeking in my whole existence—in my lodging, my
food, my clothing, and my ways of going on with

people—whatever, far from separating me from the mass of mankind, draws me nearer to them.'

Whatever else we have or have not in Count Tolstoi, we have at least a great soul and a great writer. In his Biblical exegesis, in the criticism by which he extracts and constructs his Five Commandments of Christ which are to be the rule of our lives, I find much which is questionable along with much which is ingenious and powerful. But I have neither space, nor, indeed, inclination, to criticise his exegesis here. The right moment, besides, for criticising this will come when the 'two great works,' which are in preparation, shall have appeared.

For the present I limit myself to a single criticism only—a general one. Christianity cannot be packed into any set of commandments. As I have somewhere or other said, 'Christianity is a *source;* no one supply of water and refreshment that comes from it can be called the sum of Christianity. It is a mistake, and may lead to much error, to exhibit any series of maxims, even those of the Sermon on the Mount, as the ultimate sum and formula into which Christianity may be run up.'

And the reason mainly lies in the character of the Founder of Christianity and in the nature of his utterances. Not less important than the teachings given by Jesus is the *temper* of their giver, his temper of sweetness and reasonableness, of *epieikeia.* Goethe calls him a *Schwärmer*, a fanatic ; he may much more rightly be called an opportunist. But he is an opportunist of an opposite kind from those who in politics, that 'wild and dreamlike trade' of insincerity, give themselves this name. They push or slacken, press their points hard or let them be, as may best suit the interests of their self-aggrandisement and of their party. Jesus has in view simply 'the rule of God, of the truth.' But this is served by waiting as well as by hasting forward, and sometimes served better.

Count Tolstoi sees rightly that whatever the propertied and satisfied classes may think, the

world, ever since Jesus Christ came, is judged;
'a new earth' is in prospect. It was ever in
prospect with Jesus, and should be ever in prospect with his followers. And the ideal in
prospect has to be realised. 'If ye know these
things, happy are ye if ye do them.' But they
are to be done through a great and widespread
and long-continued change, and a change of the
inner man to begin with. The most important
and fruitful utterances of Jesus, therefore, are not
things which can be drawn up as a table of stiff
and stark external commands, but the things
which have most soul in them ; because these can
best sink down into our soul, work there, set up
an influence, form habits of conduct, and prepare
the future. The Beatitudes are on this account
more helpful than the utterances from which
Count Tolstoi builds up his Five Commandments.
The very *secret* of Jesus, 'He that loveth his life
shall lose it, he that will lose his life shall save it,'
does not give us a command to be taken and
followed in the letter, but an idea to work in

our mind and soul, and of inexhaustible value
there.

Jesus paid tribute to the government and dined
with the publicans, although neither the empire
of Rome nor the high finance of Judea were compatible with his ideal and with the 'new earth'
which that ideal must in the end create. Perhaps
Levine's provisional solution, in a society like
ours, was nearer to 'the rule of God, of the truth,'
than the more trenchant solution which Count
Tolstoi has adopted for himself since. It seems
calculated to be of more use. I do not know how
it is in Russia, but in an English village the
determination of 'our circle' to earn their bread
by the work of their hands would produce only
dismay, not fraternal joy, amongst that 'majority'
who are so earning it already. 'There are plenty
of us to compete as things stand,' the gardeners,
carpenters, and smiths would say; 'pray stick
to your articles, your poetry, and nonsense; in
manual labour you will interfere with us, and be
taking the bread out of our mouths.'

So I arrive at the conclusion that Count Tolstoï has perhaps not done well in abandoning the work of the poet and artist, and that he might with advantage return to it. But whatever he may do in the future, the work which he has already done, and his work in religion as well as his work in imaginative literature, is more than sufficient to signalise him as one of the most marking, interesting, and sympathy-inspiring men of our time— an honour, I must add, to Russia, although he forbids us to heed nationality.

AMIEL [1]

IT is somewhat late to speak of Amiel, but I was late in reading him. Goethe says that in seasons of cholera one should read no books but such as are tonic, and certainly in the season of old age this precaution is as salutary as in seasons of cholera. From what I heard I could clearly make out that Amiel's Journal was not a tonic book: the extracts from it which here and there I fell in with did not much please me; and for a good while I left the book unread.

But what M. Edmond Scherer writes I do not easily resist reading, and I found that M. Scherer had prefixed to Amiel's Journal a long and im-

---

[1] Published in *Macmillan's Magazine*, September 1887.

portant introduction.   This I read; and was not less charmed by the *mitis sapientia*, the understanding, kindness and tenderness, with which the character of Amiel himself, whom M. Scherer had known in youth, was handled, than interested by the criticism on the Journal.   Then I read Mrs. Humphry Ward's interesting notice, and then— for all biography is attractive, and of Amiel's life and circumstances I had by this time become desirous of knowing more—the *Étude Biographique* of Mademoiselle Berthe Vadier.

Of Amiel's cultivation, refinement, and high feeling, of his singular graces of spirit and character, there could be no doubt.   But the specimens of his work given by his critics left me hesitating. A poetess herself, Mademoiselle Berthe Vadier is much occupied with Amiel's poetry, and quotes it abundantly.   Even Victor Hugo's poetry leaves me cold, I am so unhappy as not to be able to admire *Olympio ;* what am I to say, then, to Amiel's

'Journée
Illuminée,
Riant soleil d'avril,
En quel songe
Se plonge
Mon cœur, et que veut-il'?

But M. Scherer and other critics, who do not require us to admire Amiel's poetry, maintain that
in his Journal he has left 'a book which will not
die,' a book describing a malady of which 'the
secret is sublime and the expression wonderful';
a marvel of 'speculative intuition,' a 'psychological
experience of the utmost value.' M. Scherer and
Mrs. Humphry Ward give Amiel's Journal very
decidedly the preference over the letters of an old
friend of mine, Obermann. The quotations made
from Amiel's Journal by his critics failed, I say,
to enable me quite to understand this high praise.
But I remember the time when a new publication
by George Sand or by Sainte-Beuve was an event
bringing to me a shock of pleasure, and a French
book capable of renewing that sensation is seldom
produced now. If Amiel's Journal was of the

high quality alleged, what a pleasure to make acquaintance with it, what a loss to miss it! In spite, therefore, of the unfitness of old age to bear atonic influences, I at last read Amiel's Journal,— read it carefully through. Tonic it is not ; but it is to be read with profit, and shows, moreover, powers of great force and value, though not quite, I am inclined to think, in the exact line which his critics with one consent indicate.

In speaking of Amiel at present, after so much has been written about him, I may assume that the main outlines of his life are known to my readers : that they know him to have been born in 1821 and to have died in 1881, to have passed the three or four best years of his youth at the University of Berlin, and the remainder of his life mostly at Geneva, as a professor, first of æsthetics, afterwards of philosophy. They know that his publications and lectures, during his life-time, disappointed his friends, who expected much from his acquirements, talents, and vivacity ; and that his fame rests upon two volumes of extracts from many thousand pages of a private journal, *Journal Intime*, extending over more than thirty years, from 1848 to 1881, which he left behind him at his death. This Journal explains his sterility; and displays in explaining it, say his critics, such sincerity, with such gifts of expression and eloquence, of profound analysis and speculative intuition, as to make it most surely 'one of those books which will not die.'

The sincerity is unquestionable. As to the gifts of eloquence and expression, what are we to say? M. Scherer speaks of an 'ever new eloquence' pouring itself in the pages of the Journal: M. Paul Bourget, of 'marvellous pages' where the feeling for nature finds an expression worthy of Shelley or Wordsworth: Mrs. Humphry Ward, of 'magic of style,' of 'glow and splendour of expression,' of the 'poet and artist' who fascinates us in Amiel's prose. I cannot quite agree. Obermann has been mentioned: it seems to me that we have only to place a passage from Sénancour beside a passage from Amiel, to perceive the

difference between a feeling for nature which gives
magic to style and one which does not.   Here and
throughout I am to use as far as possible Mrs.
Humphry Ward's translation, at once spirited and
faithful, of Amiel's Journal.   I will take a passage
where Amiel has evidently some reminiscence of
Sénancour (whose work he knew well), is inspired
by Sénancour—a passage which has been extolled
by M. Paul Bourget :—

'Shall I ever enjoy again those marvellous reveries
of past days,—as, for instance, once, when I was still
quite a youth in the early dawn sitting amongst the
ruins of the castle of Faucigny ; another time in the
mountains above Lancy, under the mid-day sun, lying
under a tree and visited by three butterflies ; and
again another night on the sandy shore of the North
Sea, stretched full length upon the beach, my eyes
wandering over the Milky Way ?   Will they ever return to me, those grandiose, immortal, cosmogonic
dreams in which one seems to carry the world in one's
breast, to touch the stars, to possess the infinite ?
Divine moments, hours of ecstasy, when thought flies
from world to world, penetrates the great enigma,
breathes with a respiration large, tranquil, and profound like that of the ocean, and hovers serene and
boundless like the blue heaven !   Visits from the

Muse Urania, who traces around the foreheads of
those she loves the phosphorescent nimbus of con-
templative power, and who pours into their hearts the
tranquil intoxication, if not the authority of genius,—
moments of irresistible intuition in which a man feels
himself great as the universe and calm like God!
. . . What hours, what memories!'

And now for Obermann's turn, Obermann by
the Lake of Bienne :—

'My path lay beside the green waters of the Thiele.
Feeling inclined to muse, and finding the night so
warm that there was no hardship in being all night
out of doors, I took the road to Saint Blaise. I
descended a steep bank, and got upon the shore of
the lake where its ripple came up and expired. The
air was calm ; every one was at rest ; I remained there
for hours. Towards morning the moon shed over the
earth and waters the ineffable melancholy of her last
gleams. Nature seems unspeakably grand, when,
plunged in a long reverie, one hears the rippling of
the waters upon a solitary strand, in the calm of a night
still enkindled and luminous with the setting moon.

'Sensibility beyond utterance, charm and torment
of our vain years ; vast consciousness of a nature
everywhere greater than we are, and everywhere im-
penetrable ; all-embracing passion, ripened wisdom,
delicious self-abandonment—everything that a mortal
heart can contain of life-weariness and yearning, I felt

it all, I experienced it all, in this memorable night,
I have made a grave step towards the age of decline,
I have swallowed up ten years of life at once.   Happy
the simple, whose heart is always young !'

No translation can render adequately the ca-
dence of diction, the 'dying fall' of reveries like
those of Sénancour or Rousseau.   But even in a
translation we must surely perceive that the magic
of style is with Sénancour's feeling for nature, not
Amiel's ; and in the original this is far more manifest still.

Magic of style is creative : its possessor himself
creates, and he inspires and enables his reader in
some sort to create after him.   And creation gives
the sense of life and joy ; hence its extraordinary
value.   But eloquence may exist without magic of
style, and this eloquence, accompanying thoughts
of rare worth and depth, may heighten their effect
greatly.   And M. Scherer says that Amiel's speculative philosophy is 'on a far other scale of vastness' than Sénancour's, and therefore he gives the
preference to the eloquence of Amiel, which clothes
and conveys this vaster philosophy.   Amiel was

no doubt greatly Sénancour's superior in culture and instruction generally; in philosophical reading and what is called philosophical thought he was immensely his superior. My sense for philosophy, I know, is as far from satisfying Mr. Frederic Harrison as my sense for Hugo's poetry is from satisfying Mr. Swinburne. But I am too old to change and too hardened to hide what I think; and when I am presented with philosophical speculations and told that they are 'on a high scale of vastness,' I persist in looking closely at them and in honestly asking myself what I find to be their positive value. And we get from Amiel's powers of 'speculative intuition' things like this—

'Created spirits in the accomplishment of their destinies tend, so to speak, to form constellations and milky ways within the empyrean of the divinity; in becoming gods, they surround the throne of the sovereign with a sparkling court.'

Or this—

'Is not mind the universal virtuality, the universe latent? If so, its zero would be the germ of the infinite, which is expressed mathematically by the double zero (00).'

Or, to let our philosopher develop himself at more length, let us take this return to the zero, which Mrs. Humphry Ward prefers here to render by *nothingness* :—

'This psychological reinvolution is an anticipation of death ; it represents the life beyond the grave, the return to Scheol, the soul fading into the world of ghosts or descending into the region of *Die Mütter ;* it implies the simplification of the individual who, allowing all the accidents of personality to evaporate, exists henceforward only in the invisible state, the state of point, of potentiality, of pregnant nothingness. Is not this the true definition of mind ? is not mind, dissociated from space and time, just this ? Its development, past or future, is contained in it just as a curve is contained in its algebraical formula. This nothing is an all. This *punctum* without dimensions is a *punctum saliens.*'

French critics throw up their hands in dismay at the violence which the Germanised Amiel, propounding his speculative philosophy, often does to the French language. My objection is rather that such speculative philosophy, as that of which I have been quoting specimens has no value, is perfectly futile. And Amiel's Journal contains far too much of it.

What is futile we may throw aside; but when
Amiel tells us of his 'protean nature essentially
metamorphosable, polarisable, and virtual,' when
he tells us of his longing for 'totality,' we must
listen, although these phrases may in France, as
M. Paul Bourget says, 'raise a shudder in a
humanist trained on Livy and Pascal.' But these
phrases stood for ideas which did practically rule,
in a great degree, Amiel's life, which he often develops not only with great subtlety, but also with
force, clearness, and eloquence, making it both
easy and interesting to us to follow him. But still,
when we have the ideas present before us, I shall
ask, what is their value, what does Amiel obtain
in them for the service of either himself or other
people?

Let us take first what, adopting his own phrase,
we may call his 'bedazzlement with the infinite,'
his thirst for 'totality.' *Omnis determinatio est
negatio.* Amiel has the gift and the bent for
making his soul 'the capacity for all form, not *a*
soul but *the* soul.' He finds it easier and more

natural ' to be *man* than *a* man.' His permanent
instinct is to be ' a subtle and fugitive spirit which
no base can absorb or fix entirely.' It costs him
an effort to affirm his own personality : ' the infinite draws me to it, the *Henosis* of Plotinus intoxicates me like a philtre.'

It intoxicates him until the thought of absorp-
tion and extinction, the *Nirvâna* of Buddhism, becomes his thought of refuge :—

' The individual life is a nothing ignorant of itself,
and as soon as this nothing knows itself, individual
life is abolished in principle. For as soon as the illusion vanishes, Nothingness resumes its eternal sway,
the suffering of life is over, error has disappeared,
time and form have for this enfranchised individuality
ceased to be ; the coloured air-bubble has burst in
the infinite space, and the misery of thought has sunk
to rest in the changeless repose of all-embracing
Nothing.'

With this bedazement with the infinite and
this drift towards Buddhism comes the impatience
with all production, with even poetry and art
themselves, because of their necessary limits and
imperfection :—

'Composition demands a concentration, decision, and pliancy which I no longer possess. I cannot fuse together materials and ideas. If we are to give anything a form we must, so to speak, be the tyrants of it. We must treat our subject brutally and not be always trembling lest we should be doing it a wrong. We must be able to transmute and absorb it into our own substance. This sort of confident effrontery is beyond me ; my whole nature tends to that impersonality which respects and subordinates itself to the object ; it is love of truth which holds me back from concluding and deciding.'

The desire for the all, the impatience with what is partial and limited, the fascination of the infinite, are the topics of page after page in the Journal. It is a prosaic mind which has never been in contact with ideas of this sort, never felt their charm. They lend themselves well to poetry. but what are we to say of their value as ideas to be lived with, dilated on, made the governing ideas of life ? Except for use in passing, and with the power to dismiss them again, they are unprofitable. Shelley's

> ' Life like a dome of many-coloured glass
> Stains the white radiance of eternity
> Until death tramples it to fragments '

has value as a splendid image nobly introduced in
a beautiful and impassioned poem. But Amiel's
'coloured air-bubble,' as a positive piece of 'speculative intuition,' has no value whatever.   Nay, the
thoughts which have positive truth and value, the
thoughts to be lived with and dwelt upon, the
thoughts which are a real acquisition for our
minds, are precisely thoughts which counteract
the 'vague aspiration and indeterminate desire'
possessing Amiel and filling his Journal : they
are thoughts insisting on the need of limit, the
feasibility of performance. Goethe says admirably—

> ' Wer grosses will muss sich zusammenraffen :
> In der Beschränkung zeigt sich erst der Meister.'

' He who will do great things must pull himself
together : it is in working within limits that the
master comes out.'   Buffon says not less admirably—

> ' Tout sujet est un ; et quelque vaste qu'il soit, il
> peut être renfermé dans un seul discours.'

' Every subject is one ; and however vast it may be

is capable of being contained in a single discourse.'
The ideas to live with, the ideas of sterling value to
us, are, I repeat, ideas of this kind : ideas staunchly
counteracting and reducing the power of the infinite and indeterminate, not paralysing us with it.

And indeed we have not to go beyond Amiel
himself for proof of this. Amiel was paralysed by
living in these ideas of ' vague aspiration and indeterminate desire,' of ' confounding his personal
life in the general life,' by feeding on these ideas,
treating them as august and precious, and filling
hundreds of pages of Journal with them. He was
paralysed by it, he became impotent and miserable. And he knew it, and tells us of it himself
with a power of analysis and with a sad eloquence which to me are much more interesting
and valuable than his philosophy of Maïa and the
Great Wheel. ' By your natural tendency,' he
says to himself, ' you arrive at disgust with life,
despair, pessimism.'   And again : ' Melancholy
outlook on all sides. Disgust with myself.' And
again : ' I cannot deceive myself as to the fate in

store for me : increasing isolation, inward disappointment, enduring regrets, a melancholy neither
to be consoled nor confessed, a mournful old age,
a slow agony, a death in the desert.' And all this
misery by his own fault, his own mistakes. 'To
live is to conquer incessantly ; one must have
the courage to be happy. I turn in a vicious
circle ; I have never had clear sight of my true
vocation.'

I cannot, therefore, fall in with that particular
line of admiration which critics, praising Amiel's
Journal, have commonly followed. I cannot join
in celebrating his prodigies of speculative intuition, the glow and splendour of his beatific vision
of absolute knowledge, the marvellous pages in
which his deep and vast philosophic thought is
laid bare, the secret of his sublime malady is expressed. I hesitate to admit that all this part of
the Journal has even a very profound psychological interest : its interest is rather pathological.
In reading it we are not so much pursuing a study
of psychology as a study of mental pathology.

But the Journal reveals a side in Amiel which his critics, so far as I have seen, have hardly noticed, a side of real power, originality, and value. He says himself that he never had clear sight of his true vocation: well, his true vocation, it seems to me, was that of a literary critic. Here he is admirable: M. Scherer was a true friend when he offered to introduce him to an editor, and suggested an article on Uhland. There is hardly a literary criticism in these two volumes which is not masterly, and which does not make one desire more of the same kind. And not Amiel's literary criticism only, but his criticism of society, politics, national character, religion, is in general well informed, just, and penetrating in an eminent degree. Any one single page of this criticism is worth, in my opinion, a hundred of Amiel's pages about the Infinite Illusion and the Great Wheel. It is to this side in Amiel that I desire now to draw attention. I would have abstained from writing about him if I had only to disparage and to find fault, only to say that he had been overpraised, and that his

dealings with Maïa seemed to me profitable neither
for himself nor for others.

Let me first take Amiel as a critic of literature,
and of the literature which he naturally knew
best, French literature. Hear him as critic on
that best of critics, Sainte-Beuve, of whose death
(1869) he had just heard :—

'The fact is, Sainte-Beuve leaves a greater void
behind him than either Béranger or Lamartine ; their
greatness was already distant, historical ; he was still
helping us to think. The true critic supplies all the
world with a basis. He represents the public judgment, that is to say, the public reason, the touchstone,
the scales, the crucible, which tests the value of each
man and the merit of each work. Infallibility of
judgment is perhaps rarer than anything else, so fine
a balance of qualities does it demand—qualities both
natural and acquired, qualities of both mind and
heart. What years of labour, what study and comparison, are needed to bring the critical judgment to
maturity ! Like Plato's sage, it is only at fifty that
the critic is risen to the true height of his literary
priesthood, or, to put it less pompously, of his social
function. Not till then has he compassed all modes
of being, and made every shade of appreciation his
own. And Sainte-Beuve joined to this infinitely re-
fined culture a prodigious memory and an incredible

multitude of facts and anecdotes stored up for the
service of his thought.'

The criticism is so sound, so admirably put,
and so charming, that one wishes Sainte-Beuve
could have read it himself.

Try Amiel next on the touchstone afforded
by that 'half genius, half charlatan,' Victor
Hugo :—

'I have been again looking through Victor Hugo's
Paris (1867). For ten years event after event
has given the lie to the prophet, but the confidence
of the prophet in his own imaginings is not therefore
a whit diminished. Humility and common sense are
only fit for Lilliputians. Victor Hugo superbly
ignores everything which he has not foreseen. He
does not know that pride limits the mind, and that
a limitless pride is a littleness of soul. If he could
but learn to rank himself with other men and France
with other nations, he would see things more truly,
and would not fall into his insane exaggerations, his
extravagant oracles. But proportion and justness
his chords will never know. He is vowed to the
Titanic ; his gold is always mixed with lead, his
insight with childishness, his reason with madness.
He cannot be simple ; like the blaze of a house on
fire, his light is blinding. In short, he astonishes
but provokes, he stirs but annoys. His note is

always half or two-thirds false, and that is why he perpetually makes us feel uncomfortable. The great poet in him cannot get clear of the charlatan. A few pricks of Voltaire's irony would have made the inflation of this genius collapse, and rendered him stronger by rendering him saner. It is a public misfortune that the most powerful poet of France should not have better understood his *rôle*, and that, unlike the Hebrew prophets who chastised because they loved, he flatters his fellow-citizens from system and from pride. France is the world, Paris is France, Hugo is Paris. Bow down and worship, ye nations!'

Finally, we will hear Amiel on a consummate and supreme French classic, as perfect as Hugo is flawed, La Fontaine:—

'Went through my La Fontaine yesterday, and remarked his omissions. . . . He has not an echo of chivalry haunting him. His French history dates from Louis XIV. His geography extends in reality but a few square miles, and reaches neither the Rhine nor the Loire, neither the mountains nor the sea. He never invents his subjects, but indolently takes them ready-made from elsewhere. But with all this, what an adorable writer, what a painter, what an observer, what a master of the comic and the satirical, what a teller of a story! I am never tired of him, though I know half his fables by heart. In the matter of vocabulary, turns of expression, tones, idioms, his language is perhaps the richest of the great period, for it combines skilfully the archaic with the classical, the Gaulish element with what is French. Variety, finesse, sly fun, sensibility, rapidity, conciseness, suavity, grace, gaiety—when necessary nobleness, seriousness, grandeur—you find everything in our fabulist. And the happy epithets, and the telling proverbs, and the sketches dashed off, and the unexpected audacities, and the point driven well home! One cannot say what he has not, so many diverse aptitudes he has.

'Compare his *Woodcutter and Death* with Boileau's, and you can measure the prodigious difference between the artist and the critic who wanted to teach him better. La Fontaine brings visibly before you the poor peasant under the monarchy, Boileau but exhibits a drudge sweating under his load. The first is a historic witness, the second a school-versifier. La Fontaine enables you to reconstruct the whole society of his age; the pleasant old soul from Champagne, with his animals, turns out to be the one and only Homer of France.

'His weak side is his epicureanism, with its tinge of grossness. This, no doubt, was what made Lamartine dislike him. The religious string is wanting to his lyre, he has nothing which shows him to have known either Christianity or the high tragedies of the soul. Kind Nature is his goddess, Horace his prophet, and Montaigne his gospel. In other words, his horizon is that of the Renascence. This islet

of paganism in the midst of a Catholic society is
very curious ; the paganism is perfectly simple and
frank.'

These are but notes, jottings in his Journal,
and Amiel passed from them to broodings over the
infinite, and personality, and totality.   Probably
the literary criticism which he did so well, and for
which he shows a true vocation, gave him nevertheless but little pleasure because he did it thus
fragmentarily and by fits and starts.   To do it
thoroughly, to make his fragments into wholes, to
fit them for coming before the public, composition
with its toils and limits was necessary.   Toils and
limits composition indeed has ; yet all composition is a kind of creation, creation gives, as I have
already said, pleasure, and, when successful and
sustained, more than pleasure, joy.   Amiel, had
he tried the experiment with literary criticism,
where lay his true vocation, would have found it
so.   Sainte-Beuve, whom he so much admires,
would have been the most miserable of men if
his production had been but a volume or two of

middling poems and a journal. But Sainte-Beuve's motto, as Amiel himself notices, was that of the Emperor Severus : *Laboremus.* ' Work,' Sainte-Beuve confesses to a friend, ' is my sore burden, but it is also my great resource. I eat my heart out when I am not up to the neck in work ; there you have the secret of the life I lead.' If M. Scherer's introduction to the *Revue Germanique* could but have been used, if Amiel could but have written the article on Uhland, and followed it up by plenty of articles more !

I have quoted largely from Amiel's literary criticism, because this side of him has, so far as I have observed, received so little attention, and yet deserves attention so eminently. But his more general criticism, too, shows, as I have said, the same high qualities as his criticism of authors and books. I must quote one or two of his aphorisms : *L'esprit sert bien à tout, mais ne suffit à rien :* ' Wits are of use for everything, sufficient for nothing.' *Une société vit de sa foi et se développe par la science :* ' A society lives on its faith and develops itself by science.' *L'État libéral est irréalisable avec une religion antilibérale, et presque irréalisable avec l'absence de religion :* 'Liberal communities are impossible with an anti-liberal religion, and almost impossible with the absence of religion.' But epigrammatic sentences of this sort are perhaps not so very difficult to produce, in French at any rate. Let us take Amiel when he has room and verge enough to show what he can really say which is important about society, religion, national life and character. We have seen what an influence his years passed in Germany had upon him : we have seen how severely he judges Victor Hugo's faults : the faults of the French nation at large he judges with a like severity. But what a fine and just perception does the following passage show of the deficiencies of Germany, the advantage which the western nations have in their more finished civilisation :—

'It is in the novel that the average vulgarity of German society, and its inferiority to the societies of France and England are most clearly visible. The notion of a thing's *jarring on the taste* is wanting to German æsthetics. Their elegance knows nothing of grace; they have no sense of the enormous distance between distinction (gentlemanly, ladylike) and their stiff *Vornehmlichkeit*. Their imagination lacks style, training, education, and knowledge of the world; it is stamped with an ill-bred air even in its Sunday clothes. The race is practical and intelligent, but common and ill-mannered. Ease, amiability, manners, wit, animation, dignity, charm, are qualities which belong to others.

'Will that inner freedom of soul, that profound harmony of all the faculties, which I have so often observed among the best Germans, ever come to the surface? Will the conquerors of to-day ever civilise their forms of life? It is by their future novels that we shall be able to judge. As soon as the German novel can give us quite good society, the Germans will be in the raw stage no longer.'

And this pupil of Berlin, this devourer of German books, this victim, say the French critics, to the contagion of German style, after three hours, one day, of a *Geschichte der Æsthetik in Deutschland*, breaks out:—

'Learning and even thought are not everything. A little *esprit*, point, vivacity, imagination, grace, would do no harm. Do these pedantic books leave a single image or sentence, a single striking or new fact, in the memory when one lays them down ! No, nothing but fatigue and confusion. Oh, for clearness, terseness, brevity ! Diderot, Voltaire, or even Galiani ! A short article by Sainte - Beuve, Scherer, Renan, Victor Cherbulioz, gives one more pleasure, and makes one ponder and reflect more, than a thousand of these German pages crammed to the margin and showing the work itself rather than its result. The Germans heap the faggots for the pile, the French bring the fire. Spare me your lucubrations, give me facts or ideas. Keep your vats, your must, your dregs, to yourselves; I want wine fully made, wine which will sparkle in the glass, and kindle my spirits instead of oppressing them.'

Amiel may have been led away *deteriora sequi :* he may have Germanised until he has become capable of the verb *dépersonnaliser* and the noun *réimplication ;* but after all, his heart is in the right place : *videt meliora probatque.* He remains at bottom the man who said : *Le livre serait mon ambition.* He adds, to be sure, that it would be *son ambition,* 'if ambition were not vanity, and vanity of vanities.'

Yet this disenchanted brooder, 'full of a tran-

quil disgust at the futility of our ambitions, the
void of our existence,' bedazzled with the infinite,
can observe the world and society with consummate keenness and shrewdness, and at the same
time with a delicacy which to the man of the
world is in general wanting. Is it possible to
analyse *le grand monde*, high society, as the Old
World knows it and America knows it not, more
acutely than Amiel does in what follows?—

'In society people are expected to behave as if
they lived on ambrosia and concerned themselves
with no interests but such as are noble. Care, need,
passion, do not exist. All realism is suppressed as
brutal. In a word, what is called *le grand monde*
gives itself for the moment the flattering illusion that
it is moving in an ethereal atmosphere and breathing
the air of the gods. For this reason all vehemence,
any cry of nature, all real suffering, all heedless
familiarity, any genuine sign of passion, are startling
and distasteful in this delicate *milieu*, and at once
destroy the collective work, the cloud-palace, the im-
posing architectural creation raised by common consent. It is like the shrill cock-crow which breaks the
spell of all enchantments, and puts the fairies to flight.
These select gatherings produce without intending it
a sort of concert for eye and ear, an improvised work

of art. By the instinctive collaboration of everybody concerned, wit and taste hold festival, and the associations of reality are exchanged for the associations of imagination. So understood, society is a form of poetry; the cultivated classes deliberately recompose the idyll of the past, and the buried world of Astræa. Paradox or not, I believe that these fugitive attempts to reconstruct a dream, whose only end is beauty, represent confused reminiscences of an age of gold haunting the human heart; or rather, aspirations towards a harmony of things which every-day reality denies to us, and of which art alone gives us a glimpse.'

I remember reading in an American newspaper a solemn letter by an excellent republican, asking what were a shopman's or a labourer's feelings when he walked through Eaton or Chatsworth. Amiel will tell him : they are 'reminiscences of an age of gold haunting the human heart, aspirations towards a harmony of things which every-day reality denies to us.' I appeal to my friend the author of *Triumphant Democracy* himself, to say whether these are to be had in walking through Pittsburg.

Indeed it is by contrast with American life that *Nirvâna* appears to Amiel so desirable :—

'For the Americans, life means devouring, in-cessant activity. They must win gold, predomi-nance, power; they must crush rivals, subdue nature. They have their heart set on the means, and never for an instant think of the end. They confound being with individual being, and the expansion of self with happiness. This means that they do not live by the soul, that they ignore the immutable and eternal, bustle at the circumference of their existence because they cannot penetrate to its centre. They are restless, eager, positive, because they are super-ficial. To what end all this stir, noise, greed, struggle? It is all a mere being stunned and deafened!'

Space is failing me, but I must yet find room for a less indirect criticism of democracy than the foregoing remarks on American life :—

'*Each function to the most worthy:* this maxim is the professed rule of all constitutions, and serves to test them. Democracy is not forbidden to apply it; but Democracy rarely does apply it, because she holds, for example, that the most worthy man is the man who pleases her, whereas he who pleases her is not always the most worthy; and because she supposes that reason guides the masses, whereas in reality they are most commonly led by passion. And in the end every falsehood has to be expiated, for truth always takes its revenge.'

What publicists and politicians have to learn is, that 'the ultimate ground upon which every civilisation rests is the average morality of the masses and a sufficient amount of practical righteousness.' But where does duty find its inspiration and sanctions? In religion. And what does Amiel think of the traditional religion of Christendom, the Christianity of the Churches? He tells us repeatedly; but a month or two before his death, with death in full view, he tells us with peculiar impressiveness :—

'The whole Semitic dramaturgy has come to seem to me a work of the imagination. The apostolic documents have changed in value and meaning to my eyes. The distinction between belief and truth has grown clearer and clearer to me. Religious psychology has become a simple phenomenon, and has lost its fixed and absolute value. The apologetics of Pascal, Leibnitz, Secrétan, appear to me no more convincing than those of the Middle Age, for they assume that which is in question—a revealed doctrine, a definite and unchangeable Christianity.'

Is it possible, he asks, to receive at this day the common doctrine of a Divine Providence direct-

ing all the circumstances of our life, and consequently inflicting upon us our miseries as means
of education ?

'Is this heroic faith compatible with our actual
knowledge of the laws of nature ? Hardly. But
what this faith makes objective we may take sub-
jectively. The moral being may moralise his suffering in turning the natural fact to account for the
education of his inner man. What he cannot change
he calls the will of God, and to will what God wills
brings him peace.'

But can a religion, Amiel asks again, without miracles, without unverifiable mystery, be
efficacious, have influence with the many ? And
again he answers :—

'Pious fiction is still fiction. Truth has superior
rights. The world must adapt itself to truth, not
truth to the world. Copernicus upset the astronomy
of the Middle Age ; so much the worse for the
astronomy. The Everlasting Gospel is revolutionis-
ing the Churches ; what does it matter ?'

This is water to our mill, as the Germans say,
indeed. But I have come even thus late in the
day to speak of Amiel, not because I found him
supplying water for any particular mill, either

mine or any other, but because it seemed to me
that by a whole important side he was eminently
worth knowing, and that to this side of him the
public, here in England at any rate, had not
had its attention sufficiently drawn. If in the
seventeen thousand pages of the Journal there
are many pages still unpublished in which
Amiel exercises his true vocation of critic, of
literary critic more especially, let his friends give
them to us, let M. Scherer introduce them to us,
let Mrs. Humphry Ward translate them for us.
But *sat patriæ Priamoque datum :* Maïa has had
her full share of space already : I will not ask for
a word more about the infinite illusion, or the
double zero, or the Great Wheel.

THE END

Printed in Great Britain by R. & R. CLARK, LIMITED, *Edinburgh.*